TWO WEEKS IN KENYA

Cora Lee.
it was great meeting you at
the Bianco's!
Thank you f your loving Support

Peace
Michael Schneider

TWO WEEKS IN KENYA

A Story of Poverty and Hope

Michael Schneiders

To order additional copies of this book, contact:
Xlibris Corporation
1-888-795-4274
www.Xlibris.com
Orders@Xlibris.com
32620

CONTENTS

To Patti, Mike, and Megan

We make a living by what we get; we make a life by what we give.

—Winston Churchill

Preface

Visiting Kenya for the first time stirred many personal feelings that have slowly been bubbling to the surface for a very long time. I have never been someone who has felt comfortable in my surroundings. Always telling myself that their must be something more. We all have had these feelings at one time or another. Some call it a midlife crisis. And whether or not we want to believe that the crisis is real, well, I believe it is.

My fear is that at the end of the day, can I honestly say that I made a difference in someone's life? Was my effort sufficient? Have I left something here that others can build upon? Time is a very interesting concept. It is the only thing that makes us all equal, twenty-four hours in a day; and once it's gone, it's gone. Like your youth, you cannot get it back. What separates us all is what we do with those few hours we have. Time separates the wheat from the chafe.

So why write a book? There are already many books written about Africa that tell of the trouble and despair. As I was growing up, books were my refuge. They helped me feel comfortable with myself and who I wanted to be (although I must admit I don't know exactly what that is yet).

As I became older, books became my true lover. The written word, to me, is exciting, sexy, and sensual like a beautiful woman or a great bottle of wine. They are all related. Pleasing to the senses, an opportunity to lose oneself in a magical way.

The last five to ten years have been pivotal in my forty-four years on earth. Those years have changed my entire thought process on the meaning of peace and the need to help one another. My life has become much more than the little towns I grew up in and the one I now call my home. The older generations in those little towns challenged all of us growing up there to be better, caring, color-blind people because none of us wanted to be like them.

After I returned from Kenya, I was quite frankly glad to be home. There is a lot to be said for the comfort of your own bed and the ability to drink water straight from the tap. But soon afterward, I was ready to return.

Many of my friends were perplexed. "Why on earth would you want to go back there?" I could understand their question. Why would anyone want to go back to a country where there is disease and dying, where you have to boil all your water, and where most of the time you have to take a crap in a hole in the ground?

Somehow, I found Kenya to be a place where I could finally feel comfortable with myself. It was a place where I found friendship, comfort, and compassion. A place where every single day I could count my blessings.

My purpose in writing this book is to tell a story, hopefully a compelling one, of another people so different from us but also so much like ourselves. I hope that you will gain a little snapshot into their lives. I hope that many of you will see yourself in some part of this story, enough for you to say, "I want to help these people."

This book would not have come together without the efforts and encouragement of many people. My wife, Patti, was so important in this effort; first, she encouraged me to go to Kenya and then put up with me locked in our spare bedroom, writing and researching this project.

Many thanks to Gina Baker, my sister-in-law, with whom I shared snippets of the text along the way, and her encouragement kept me going.

If we are lucky, someone will come into our lives who will change its path forever. That person for me is Father Pat Stephenson. His odd humor, down-to-earth view on life, and constant and gentle prodding to always see the world from a different perspective has changed my life forever.

In June of 2005, Father Pat was diagnosed with colon cancer. Because he had a routine colonoscopy, the cancer was found very early; and within six weeks of his surgery, he had fully recovered.

As is so indicative of his personality, he felt that it was a blessing that he had contracted cancer. Father Pat believes that it has made him a better priest by experiencing the anxiety, stress, and surgery. He feels that he can now better relate to those who have life-threatening medical conditions. This story about Kenya is as much his as it is mine.

Davina Rubin—a retired schoolteacher from Napa, California, and a frequent contributor to *Napa Valley Life* magazine—helped fix some serious technical issues that only a fresh eye could find.

But this book would not have been possible without the coaching, teaching, and patience of Kari Ruel, owner of Choice Publishing and publisher of *Napa Valley Life* magazine. She served as my editor, coach, research assistant, agent, and everything else during this project. She prodded me to take the voluminous number of journal entries I had made during the trip and write them in story form. This book would have never made it into publication without her. Kari also shot the author's photo and edited all the photos in this book.

All other photos in this book were taken by me or, in the case where I am in the photo, by either Father Pat Stephenson, Tom Wahome, or Sister Mary Theresa.

Introduction

W hat the hell did I know about Africa? What the hell does anyone know about Africa? AIDS, death, and tribal warfare—it's rare to hear or read anything positive about sub-Saharan Africa.

Being raised in the 1960s, my vision of Africa was formed by Marlin Perkins and his show, *Mutual of Omaha's Wild Kingdom*, and from *National Geographic* magazines. Every Sunday night, Marlin Perkins would send his assistant, Jim, into the African bush to roust out some wild animal while Marlin hid behind a tree. Africa became, to me, a vast dry, dusty wilderness full of wild animals and wild people.

I used to love to sneak a peek at *National Geographic*. On occasion, they would print colored photos of topless jungle women and bottomless jungle men carrying spears and shields, bouncing around a campfire to the beating of tribal drums. It was quite exciting for an eight-year-old to catch a glimpse of the photos of the dancing black breasts of those jungle women. It created an image of an amazing alien world to me.

Africa was the "dark continent" to me. I can remember asking myself, "How could people live like that when we had nice clothes to wear and a grocery store to purchase our food?" I just could not imagine hunting for my daily meal with a spear.

I was born in Rodeo, California, and raised among the Italian Catholics in the neighboring town of Crockett. The combined population of these two towns was less than six thousand. This was conservative, sheltered small-town America. So in 2002, when Father Pat Stephenson—the pastor of my Catholic parish in American Canyon, California—said he was going to Kenya on a safari, I said to him, "Oh, that's so wonderful"; but I was thinking, *Better you than me. Your ponytail must be pulled too tight. Why don't you go to some Caribbean island and sit on the beach for two weeks instead? The rum must be better in the Caribbean.*

When he returned to American Canyon, I figured I would at least show some interest in his trip. I eagerly looked forward to some Marlin Perkins—type stories about the wild animals of the Maasai Mara of Kenya.

He didn't disappoint me but did surprise the hell out of me because although Father Pat's tales did have all the elements I expected to hear about the wild animals of Africa, about predators and prey, the struggle for survival, and the never-ending search for food, he was not telling me about the animals at all; he was talking about the street children of Nairobi.

When the group from his safari excursion took a short break in Kenya's capital, Nairobi, Father Pat thought it would give him an opportunity to do some sightseeing.

After hiring a cab and arranging for the driver to show him the city, he was not happy to see that the cab did not have air-conditioning. It had just rained, and the humidity was suffocating. He felt very warm and his ponytail, which was tucked under his pink bandana, was soaked with sweat.

As Father Pat rode through the steamy streets of Nairobi, his thoughts drifted toward a bottle of Tusker, the local Kenyan brew; but he was jolted back to reality by what he saw.

In the streets of Nairobi, Father Pat saw hundreds of children half clothed, living under cars and begging for money. He saw young girls selling their bodies so they could provide a few shillings[1] for their families. Many of these teenage girls had children of their own.

There were many reasons that these street children of Nairobi had been abandoned, but the underlying cause of it all was poverty. Their parents were either too poor to take care of them or they had died from, or were too sick with AIDS. Father Pat was so taken with what he saw he cancelled a scheduled hot-air balloon ride and donated the cost of five hundred dollars to a local church instead.

Upon his return, Father Pat also told me that since he left Nairobi, all he could think about were those street kids; and he knew someday he would return to find out how he could help.

Because of the emotion he expressed when he told me about these kids, I told him, never expecting him to ever ask me, that if he ever went back to Kenya, I would like to go with him.

This is how I—you know, the one who would rather be on the beach on some Caribbean island—found myself traveling to Kenya.

One Saturday evening in October 2003, my wife, Patti, and I were attending a social event in American Canyon. Before dinner, Father Pat was working the room with his steady traveling companion, a tall glass of Beefeater gin on the rocks. He came over to our table and said, "By Christmas, the parish will have collected five

---

[1] Kenyan money is called the Kenyan shilling. One U.S. dollar equals about seventy-five Kenyan shillings.

grand for Kenya. I'm going back in January to deliver the money in person, and by the way, you're going with me." This put me in a very difficult position because when I had told him before that I wanted to go with him next time, I hadn't meant it.

But Father Pat had presented me with an enormous opportunity. I could be that explorer from *National Geographic* that I had read about so many times in the magazines. How could I not go? Hell, maybe I would get to see those dancing black breasts in person!

There were several things I had to consider before agreeing to go to Kenya: Could I get the time off from work? Would my wife, Patti, let me go? What about safety? There had been a State Department travel advisory regarding Kenya for several years. Third-world countries are dangerous.

It took about a week to make my decision. Patti and I were at my son's soccer game, and all I could think about was traveling to Kenya.

It was evident to everyone at the game that I was distracted because I was not harassing the referees or making smart-ass comments about the coaching. Patti smiled, reached over, grabbed my hand, and asked me if I was all right.

Patti has a great smile; and her beautiful brown eyes, the same brown color as her sexy mocha Sicilian complexion, just twinkle in the sunlight. She squeezed my hand and said, "You're going to Kenya, aren't you?" Her soft touch brought me back to reality. "Yes," I replied.

I decided to leave the travel arrangements up to Father Pat. The next day, he called his travel agent, and we were booked. The trip would start in San Francisco, lay over in London for eight hours, and then finish up in Nairobi. Total travel time would be twenty-eight hours, not counting the three-hour preflight wait in San Francisco.

I was dying to learn more about Kenya. So before the trip, I turned to today's modern encyclopedia: the Internet. Within fifteen minutes, I knew how and where to apply for a visa and how much of a pin cushion I would become with all the vaccinations I would need.

The Center for Disease Control (CDC)[2] has one killer Web site—that is, if you want to read about all the things that can kill you. The Kenyan government does not require vaccinations; but you would be crazy not to protect yourself against the diseases listed by the CDC: polio, meningitis, typhoid, yellow fever, hepatitis, and malaria.

A couple of weeks later, I was in the shot clinic at the local hospital to get my vaccinations. I received three shots in one arm and three shots in the other.

Seizing the opportunity of being in the care of a brown-skinned, glistening-red-lipsticked twenty-something Jennifer Lopez look-alike, I tried to get her to give me two shots in my right arm, two in my left arm, and two in my ass. My full-figured Jennifer nurse laughed at me and said, "All you guys keep trying to take your pants off in here!"

---

[2]   www.cdc.gov

My visit to the hospital was a great example of why you should always ask questions. The nurse kept asking me, after every shot, if I wanted all the shots at once.

"Hell yes!" I said. It's not like I was having so much fun that I wanted to go back and do it all over again.

Just before each shot, the nurse would say, "This one might make you sick." I was thinking, *Shut up already*, but I should have asked her why she kept asking.

That evening, while Patti and I were enjoying dinner at our favorite Chinese restaurant, I broke out in a cold sweat and began to feel light-headed. These symptoms are usually caused by the Kung Pao, but I had not ordered it that night. I had a 102-degree fever for a few hours, and I felt like I had the flu.

In the morning, after a good night's sleep, I felt much better and decided to read the information the nurse gave me the previous day. On the very first page, it said, "Do not take all your vaccinations in the same day. A high fever and flulike symptoms may occur." I sat there on the edge of my chair, slapped my forehead with my right palm, and murmured, "What a dumbass!"

Next up was applying to the Kenyan government for a visa. Requesting a visa requires a travel visa form, passport, two extra passport photos, a copy of my flight itinerary, return postage, and a fifty-dollar processing fee.

The Kenyan Embassy in Washington DC processed my visa quickly, and I had my passport back within a week. Since the Kenyan economy depends on the tourist trade, I did not expect any problems.

Father Pat did run into a few problems because he had lost his passport. It was amusing watching him scramble around at the last minute.

He paid an extra fee to get his replacement passport within three days. He then sent it on to the Kenyan Embassy with an extra twenty dollars, hoping that the "tip" would help get his paperwork processed quickly. Within a week, the twenty dollars was returned along with his passport and his visa to Kenya.

Before leaving on any trip, I look for a travel book that would give me the tips and tricks that I would need to be safe, healthy, and have a good time. I recommend The Lonely Planet series of books because they are written from firsthand accounts and include history and cultural advice. Knowing how to say please, thank you, and to be able to ask where the bathroom is can be very helpful.

So I did travel to Nairobi with Father Pat. When I read about Kenya and its people before the trip, I realized that this was not a country or people that could be experienced secondhand. I needed to go there and find out for myself.

My expectations of what we would find in Kenya were conflicted by my early television exposure and my recent research about Kenya. But as our journey evolved, what I did find was despair, hope, tragedy, compassion, and humanity at its groveling worst and at its heavenly best. Kenya is a complex combination of contrast, abundant life, and sudden death.

Come, journey with me as we spend two weeks in Kenya.

Chapter 1

Getting There

P atti and I were celebrating Christmas 2003 with our two kids and friends in Seattle. I was enjoying an Irish coffee in the restaurant at Stevens Pass Ski Resort.

Wispy snow so white it looked blue fell in swirls around us. It had been a great day; and it was easy to forget about everything of consequence until, to my frustration, my cell phone rang. My intention was to leave the damn thing in the car. But there it was, playing Mozart's aria in my pocket. I had no idea how it survived since I spent the entire day falling down on it while trying to ski.

"Yo, dog!" It was Father Pat. *Dog* is *God* spelled backward.

Father Pat is not your proper, stiff-collared, holier-than-thou priest. He never wears the traditional black uniform of a Roman Catholic priest but wears the same blue outfit that he wore in the air force. Actually, he rarely wears the Roman collar outside of church, and when he is asked what he does for a living, he describes himself as a teacher.

"It keeps people from 'weirding' out on me," he said. More importantly, we got along so well because he was a smart-ass just like me.

At sixty-three years old, he was having the time of his life, tending to our small parish. When I met him five years ago, he had been retired for a couple of years as a "full bird" colonel from the United States Air Force. Father Pat sports a beard and a ponytail.

"Did you hear?" he said.

"Hear what?" I asked.

"The travel warnings, dog. Flights being canceled . . . State Department warnings about possible terrorism in Kenya."

Earlier in the week, the United States government had reissued a travel warning to Kenya. Flights were also cancelled from France to Washington DC and to Los Angeles. It was the first time that United States intelligence had cancelled or delayed flights because of possible terrorist threats.

"So? Are you still going?" I asked.

"Yep," Father Pat said without hesitation.

"So am I."

"See ya when you get back, dog."

"Okay."

That conversation was vintage Father Pat—short abbreviated sentences—but I have come to understand his lingo. I also knew what was on his mind. In 1998, the American Embassy in Nairobi had been blown to bits by a car bomb planted by an Islamic member of Osama Bin Laden's al Qaeda terrorist organization. Two hundred fifteen Kenyans were killed, and over four thousand people were injured.

When our snowy Christmas vacation ended a few days later, I had a quick turnaround. We came home; I unpacked, repacked, and left for Kenya the following day.

*   *   *

As I walked the couple of blocks from my house to Father Pat's, a half hour before we were to leave for San Francisco International Airport, I realized that I did not know where we were going to stay in Nairobi. I usually liked the unexpected, but in this case, not knowing made me a little nervous.

Father Pat had no idea either; so that morning, just to cover our bases, he booked us a room at the Norfolk Hotel in Nairobi.

Then just as we were heading out the door, Father Pat received a phone call from someone in Nairobi, letting us know that we had received an official invitation to stay at the J. J. McCarthy Convent in Nairobi as guests of Archbishop Rafael S. Ndingi Mwana'a Nzeki. I felt much better now because that meant that Sister Mary Theresa must have also received our e-mail containing our flight information.

About an hour later, we arrived at the San Francisco International Airport. We gave ourselves a little extra time because we expected to experience extremely tight security at the airport. At first, we were surprised to find nothing unusual. We checked in; went through security; took off our shoes, belts; emptied our pockets; and off we went.

We had about two hours before our flight, and I could hear "Johnny Walker," my favorite scotch, calling my name; so we looked for a quiet place to have a drink. At the end of the international terminal, we found an empty bar. It was the perfect place to relax and talk about the housing arrangements.

While I sipped a Johnny Walker and Father Pat nursed his Beefeater gin, we decided that moving from the Norfolk Hotel to the convent was not a done deal.

There were a few conditions that would have to be met, such as safety, running water, Western bathrooms, general comfort, and privacy.

After our second drink, we decided to head to the gate. This is where security became a pain in the ass. After being directed to a holding area and kept like cattle, each passenger was called forward one by one. I drew a female security guard named Bertha "the Beast Master." Bertha checked in at about five foot eight, 220 pounds. She had short greasy black hair, and there were still crumbs from lunch clinging to her chin hairs. She demanded that I take off my coat, belt, and shoes. I had to empty my pockets and the entire contents of my backpack onto her table. Her fat greasy fingers were quite skilled at the full-body search. After checking to make sure that my "family jewels" were still intact, I boarded British Airways.

Meeting up with Father Pat on the Jetway, he said that he had only received a quick pat down.

As we squished in our coach seats, the pilot brought the Rolls Royce—manufactured engines to life; and we were quickly airborne, heading east on the first leg of our journey.

We were both hungry, and I was overjoyed to see the dinner cart making its way down the aisle. Chicken or beef with a bad French wine were our choices. I just can't enjoy any bottle of wine that has a screw top.

I don't know if it was nerves, excitement, or the infamous British cuisine; but it was a miracle that I was able to keep the rubbery and tasteless chicken down. After sitting in my stomach for a short time, it began torturing me like an out-of-tune country singer with a lisp.

I had talked to a few people that had been to Africa, and everyone told me that we would get sick in Nairobi. Here I was getting sick before I left the United States airspace.

Father Pat sat next to a British couple. The bulbous-nosed, pitted-faced Max became my hero because at no time during the eleven-hour flight did he get up from his window seat. Ida, his wife, was sitting in the center seat next to Father Pat. She appeared to be a petite woman, but little did we know what was lurking below the armrest.

After dinner, Father Pat tried to settle into a comfortable position and get some sleep. His neighbor, Ida, made it quite impossible. She had propped her enormous ass on the armrest between her seat and Father Pat's seat. It was a half-moon arrangement with the armrest separating the moon; so every time he moved in his seat or turned his head to the right, he was confronted with Ida's huge—well, you get the picture. At one point, Father Pat leaned in my direction and howled like a dog. He was howling at Ida's moon.

My stomach finally settled down just in time for the second meal. What luck! Packed in a very cute box was a stale croissant smeared with mayonnaise—which, I'm sure, was rescued from the *Titanic*—and a sulfurous-smelling green-tinted boiled egg. I drank the juice and passed on the rest.

During the flight, there was this cute, little five-year-old girl, with big brown eyes and pigtails, named Amanda sitting three seats to my left. She was a perfect little girl. Amanda either slept or played with her dolls for most of the trip, but she must have had a bad encounter with the excellent British Airways cuisine. Almost on queue, when the rear wheels of the plane touched down, she heaved her dinner and whatever else was in her stomach all over her clothes, on the seat in front of her, and on her father's pants and shoes.

After an upset stomach and not being able to sleep, I was so happy to arrive in London. It was rainy and cold, but the fifty-degree temperature outside felt amazingly refreshing. The dirty, moist air of London was a relief compared to the warm, recycled air of the airplane. Fatigue had begun to set in, and we still had an eight-hour layover and another nine-hour fight ahead of us. But things started to look up when we left the airport by taxi to the Green Man.[3]

The Green Man.

The Green Man is an authentic English pub just a few miles from the airport. The original owner, Nicholas Hurst, poured the first glass of ale at the Green Man in 1602. It was built with the timbers of decommissioned ships from Portsmouth. The beams that crossed the interior were over one thousand years old.

I couldn't wait for a beer. I was hoping the Green Man served Guinness Stout, and they did. One has to love watching Guinness Stout pouring into a glass. Guinness is not a dark beer; it is a black beer, and it does not actually *pour* into a glass; it *flows* into a glass. If one pours a Guinness properly, it creates rich dark foam that looks as if it defies gravity because the silky, sandlike foam rises from the bottom of the glass to the top.

After our second Guinness, we headed back to the main terminal at London's Heathrow Airport. It was time to find a couple of empty seats in the waiting area and get some sleep. Father Pat took over a row of seats and, using his backpack as a pillow, fell fast asleep.

I was drifting peacefully off to dreamland when I was jolted back to consciousness by an enormously obese woman chasing her eleven-year-old son around the airport. She was screaming at the top of her lungs as every inch of her squat torso wiggled

---

[3]   www.thegreenmanbedfont.co.uk

comically down the terminal after him. The boy was enjoying every minute of it. Finally, he headed toward the far end of the terminal, and when everyone in our area finished laughing, I was able to catch a short nap.

Before we knew it, our flight was announced; and after a short wait at the gate, we were in the air. I felt like I had been up for a week. The bags under my eyes were so big I wasn't sure if security would let me carry them on the airplane.

As the rear wheels left the tarmac, I was asleep. I could have slept through a nuclear bomb. I know that is not the best image when flying, but it was true.

On this flight, I did not mind missing the British Airways' gourmet cooking because they were serving the same damn chicken and beef. I slept soundly for about four hours. When I woke up, it was dark outside, except for the island of Sicily.

Sicily sparkled like a newly polished jewel. The outline of this gem was ringed in lights with spots of lighted civilization scattered about its interior. I wondered how many old men were down there, sitting around a handcrafted wooden table, drinking homemade red wine from jelly jars.

Although my brain wanted to see more, my eyes would not allow it; and I fell into a deep sleep. The next thing I remembered was the sound of the captain's voice announcing that we would soon begin our descent into Nairobi.

Our descent was spectacular: huge cotton-candy clouds rose like white and gray towers on each side of the aircraft. We seemed to be playing hide-and-seek with the sun, never going through the clouds, only around them.

It was just after sunrise. For a while, all I could see were the tops of the clouds. As the airplane banked right, I caught a glimpse of Mount Kenya's peak basking proudly in the sunshine.

We broke clear of the clouds a few thousand feet above the northern end of the Rift Valley. My eyes strained, but could not see, the animals for which Africa is so famous. Finally, we glided safely to the ground. We were "in country." It was already Wednesday. What the hell happened to Tuesday? Damn, that was a long trip.

Chapter 2

First Look at Nairobi

Usually, hitting the ground is the last thing you want to think about when flying; but having been sealed in a metal tube, traveling six-hundred-plus miles per hour for nineteen of the last twenty-seven hours, I felt like it was wonderful to hit the ground. I wanted to run off the airplane and kiss the tarmac.

Kenyatta International Airport is old, small, unorganized, and smelled like my grandmother's basement: musty and damp. Dusty faded yellow walls, torn wall paper, and chipped linoleum-tiled floors (full of asbestos, no doubt) greeted us everywhere we went.

The airport was named after the first Kenyan president, Jomo Kenyatta, who became president in December of 1963 and ruled until his death in 1978. Kenyatta was an early leader in Kenya's struggle for independence from the British. He spent nearly seven years in prison for his role in the rebellion, which the locals call the Mau Mau. Although the British quashed the Mau Mau, the wheels had been put into motion for Kenya's independence.

According to local newspaper reports, Kenyatta's obsessive favoritism shown to his own Kikuyu tribe caused many problems within his government and with the other tribes in Kenya. Laws were created that benefited only the Kikuyu, and he filled most of the government posts with members of the Kikuyu tribe. Kenya's government started out with the goal that their country would be represented by all Kenyans, but it soon became a country ruled by the Kikuyu.

It became very dangerous to oppose Kenyatta's power. Those who did vanished. Although Kenya became a prosperous nation under Kenyatta, his last few years were marred by charges of nepotism and corruption.

As I was walking through the airport, it became apparent that anyone could get a visa to enter Kenya at the airport because government officials were giving them out like candy. There were over two hundred people from our flight, standing in line to get their visa. It wasn't a line but actually a mob. It reminded me of a herd of wildebeasts migrating from Tanzania to the Maasai Reserve in northern Kenya. The last person in line must have spent three hours waiting their turn.

There was a large sign hanging from the ceiling above the customs desk instructing visitors to report to the police any corruption or any government official demanding a bribe. This was an indication that Kenya was beginning to recover from twenty-three years of violence and corruption under the leadership of Daniel Toroitich arap Moi. Moi, who quickly succeeded Kenyatta as the president of Kenya and became known as the "king of corruption." He was accused by his opposition of pocketing millions of dollars that had been sent by other nations to help Kenya.

It was under the inept rule of Moi that AIDS took hold and spread like wildfire. His government would not recognize AIDS as the killer disease it was, and according to the locals I spoke to, the government tried to hide it. There was no medical care available for AIDS patients and no education on how to prevent the disease. We heard horror stories of men who believed that they could be cured of AIDS by having sex with virgins and that oral sex would not spread the virus. I would guess that when you match that with the amount of teenage prostitution I witnessed in the cities and small villages, the disease quickly became uncontrollable.

Official government statistics put Kenya's AIDS infection rate at 15 percent. AIDS-infected Kenyans are often thrown out on the streets by their own families and sometimes stoned to death. Because of the stigma, the lack of education, and the ignorance of the people, it is estimated that four to five cases of AIDS go unreported. In a city like Nairobi, with 3.5 million citizens, the number of AIDS infections could be over 60 percent, or about the entire population of Los Angeles.

For Moi's crimes against the people of Kenya, the new government not only allowed him to join the government but also gave him amnesty in a crazy attempt to heal the nation. He essentially received a free pass.

*   *   *

The line through customs was short because of all the people filling out their entry visa paperwork. Our agent was a young black man. Dressed nattily in a blue sweater and gray slacks, he had a bright, welcoming big smile that immediately made me feel at home. His smile also helped distract from his eyes that not only pointed in different directions but also seemed to operate independently of each other. After carefully inspecting our passports and with each eye revolving in different directions, he allowed us to pass.

Heading to the baggage claim area, we could see that only passengers and armed military personnel were allowed in the area. Make no mistake about it; this airport was not a place to fool around in. The place was crawling with heavily armed AK-47-packing army men. This sight was very unnerving and an early sign that we were at the beginning of a journey that was way beyond our comfort zone.

The soldiers' dark green uniforms blended so well with their black skin that they reminded me of the little green army men I used to play with as a kid.

Father Pat, with his pink bandana, drew quite a bit of attention, not because he was a priest—no one knew that yet—but because everything we had seen so far was the color of dirt. Pink stuck out.

He decided to go outside to see if Sister Mary Theresa had arrived while I waited for the luggage. After several minutes, he returned without finding anyone to pick us up. Father Pat was beginning to sweat. He was sure no one was coming to get us.

At the baggage claim, the turnstile quickly filled with luggage because the wildebeests were still back in the terminal, waiting for their visas. One by one, our bags dropped onto the conveyor.

While we were removing our bags from the turnstile, one of the AK-47—packing green army men came over. His pitch-black skin and very square features made him look like a cartoon character, but the AK-47 on his shoulder made him very real.

Mr. AK-47 took a keen interest in Father Pat. He wanted to know who Father Pat was, whom he was with, and why he was in Kenya. Mr. AK-47 never looked at or talked to me. Were my feelings hurt? Hell no! I was looking for a place to hide.

His commanding black eyes focused on our luggage. He pointed at one of our bags with a finger that looked amazing like a big, fat black banana. Mr. AK-47 wanted to know what was in it.

The situation was starting to get ugly, and Mr. AK-47 began treating us like we were on the Kenyan military's most-wanted list. I now understood how a black person in the United States felt when a cop pulls them over for DWB: driving while black. We were RLWW: retrieving luggage while white.

As I was moving our luggage to a place where it could be inspected, I was starting to have visions of being marched off to some flesh-rotting dungeon. Father Pat casually mentioned that we were in Kenya as guests of the archbishop of Nairobi. Mr. AK-47 immediately backed off and left us alone. We had been told by Sister Mary Theresa how powerful a man Archbishop Ndingi was; we just got a glimpse of that power.

Free from the Kenyan army, we headed out of the airport and were greeted by Sister Mary Theresa. She had been outside the airport all along and had seen Father Pat and his pink bandana but had been unable to get to the front of the crowd to catch his attention. She quickly shook hands with us and carried all six of our bags to the parking lot by herself. It's fair, at this point, to ask, why would she carry all of our bags by herself? It was because we were guests in her country, and the people of Kenya treat their guests like royalty. She was also stubborn as hell, and she refused to let me help her.

Sister Mary Theresa is the development director for the Catholic Archdiocese[4] of Nairobi and is in charge of all the programs that are designed to help the people rise from poverty and become contributing members of their community. Her duties also include HIV/AIDS education and prevention for the kids of the archdiocese.

She is the perfect person for the job. At sixty-five years old, Sister Mary Theresa looks and acts more like thirty-five. It is difficult to say no to her, and if you did, she wouldn't accept it. This is one tough broad responsible for five million people in her diocese.

Leaving the airport was an adrenaline rush. It felt for the first time like I was in Africa. It was warm and tropical. The smell of jet fuel and car exhaust filled the air. It was about eight o'clock in the morning, and it was beautiful in Nairobi. Artistic clouds and warm sunshine would entertain us the entire day. I looked around and thought, *Hell, where were the natives? The spears? The animals? I'm in Africa, damn it!* But things were still very different.

Everything we had seen so far was reversed from my comfortable little world. The white people were standing in long lines for their visas and travel information while the black people were enforcing the rules. This was going to be an interesting two weeks.

Making our way through the parking lot, we found Tom Wahome waiting for us. He would be our driver for the duration of our trip. Tom looked like he was ready to play golf, dressed in khakis and a polo shirt. He was forty-eight years old, tall, thin, and black with closely cropped hair; and he carried a prayer book wherever he went. Tom turned out to be a perfect match for us. He spoke excellent English and was just as much a smart-ass as we were.

Father Pat, Tom, and me.

We would be traveling in a Toyota Land Cruiser donated to the archdiocese by the United Nations.

After Sister Mary Theresa packed our bags into the Land Cruiser, we finally had a chance to properly greet her. We broke with Kenyan custom and gave her a big hug. In

---

4   The Catholics divide up countries into smaller areas called diocese. An archdiocese is the head diocese of a specified region. It's like a business that has sales offices all over the country. The archdiocese is like the company's headquarters.

Kenya, it is customary for everyone to greet one another with a handshake. Even the women shake hands with each other. Hugs and kisses, or any sign of public affection, are reserved for married people. After hugging Sister Mary Theresa, I proclaimed, within earshot of several strangers, "We must be married now!"

*   *   *

Damn, there were black people everywhere! I don't know what the hell I expected. After all, we were in Africa. I looked around and started to laugh. I had to explain why to Father Pat because he was looking at me like I had lost my mind.

"Remember what Bernadette told us a couple of weeks ago?" I said.

Bernadette was a friend of Father Pat's who grew up in Kenya and now lived in American Canyon. We would be visiting some of her family on this trip.

"No," he said.

"She said, 'Just relax and blend in.' How the hell do we blend in?"

Then we both started to laugh.

For the next twelve days, Father Pat and I saw no more than six people (except at the Norfolk Hotel) that weren't black. We were the minority, and it quickly made me feel out of place. I was not sure how we would be treated. This trip would be a test of my conviction that people are just people no matter what color they are.

*   *   *

Our trip to the Norfolk Hotel did not look any different than traveling through inner-city neighborhoods in Detroit or Philadelphia. There were trashy, faded, run-down buildings and hundreds of black people milling around. Shopkeepers had steel roll-up doors above the entrances of their businesses.

On our way to the hotel, I noticed that my armpits were screaming for a shower; but I blended in quite nicely. When you're in a city where over a million people are trying to figure out how to survive day to day, personal hygiene is not high on their list of priorities. Our traveling group would wait for us in the restaurant at the Norfolk Hotel while Father Pat and I checked in and cleaned up.

The Norfolk Hotel first opened its doors on Christmas Day 1904 and quickly became known for its elegance and comfort. During British colonial rule in Kenya, it was where the British upper class would stay. Today it is one of the favorite places for Americans and Europeans to stay when traveling on safari.

Two bellboys met us at our car and helped us with our luggage. They were both no older than sixteen years old, very polite, and spoke broken English. Father Pat and I tipped them both eight hundred Kenyan shillings, which was a little over ten U.S. dollars. This was nearly two weeks' salary for the bellboys. They were quite grateful and could not stop saying, "Asante sana," which means thank you in Swahili.

As we walked through the lush courtyard to our room, we could not help but notice the white, blue, and orange orchids; banana trees; and elephant ear plants. I was thinking that it would take quite a bit to move us to the convent.

Our room was old but clean. The walls were a mix of plaster and oak paneling. Paintings depicting hunting scenes and African animals hung on the walls. A dark-wood entertainment center housing a twenty-five-inch Sony television sat in the corner. The room had a red-and-brown couch and two single-sized beds.

The bathroom was all oak paneling, with a shower stall. Of course, none of this made any difference. It was a hot shower I wanted. It felt like heaven. Clean and smeared with deodorant, Father Pat and I headed down to the Lord Delamere Restaurant at the Norfolk.

The restaurant was located to the left of the entrance to the hotel. The patio was decorated with gray tables, padded chairs, and was covered with a newly thatched rectangular roof. Our table had a nice view of Harry Thuker Road, which runs in front of the hotel.

We were treated to a feast of fruits, eggs, toast, and french fries. Tea, coffee, fruit juice, Coca-Cola, and Orange Fanta were available to quench our thirst. I wasted no time stuffing myself. I was so hungry I could have eaten the goat that was grazing across the street. Little did I know, later in the trip, I would be eating goat.

Agnes, the sister of Father Pat's friend Bernadette, and Agnes's daughters, Judy and Winnie, joined us at the restaurant for lunch.

Agnes is a vibrant, active, and strong-willed seventy-one-year-old. She is a retired schoolteacher and headmaster. When you meet her for the first time, you just can't help notice her enormous breasts. Let's just say that you would never catch Agnes jumping rope. She taught and supervised in most of the public schools in Machakos.[5]

Agnes's thirty-three-year-old daughter Florence, Agnes, and Father Pat.

Although Agnes had lived previously in the United States, I knew little about her. She told me that she lived in a small house on a hillside with no running water and no electricity in the old British trading post of Machakos.

---

[5] Machakos is a city located about thirty miles southeast of Nairobi.

Life in Kenya, for most people, is simple and difficult at the same time. Only 30 percent of the buildings have running water. In those that do, residents still have to boil their water before drinking it.

Water is tricky for Westerners. Was that piece of fruit washed with bad water? How about those ice cubes? You could drive yourself crazy worrying about it all the time, but it is important that you do so. Intestinal parasites and cholera are big problems not only in the small towns but in the big cities as well.

I was having a wonderful time talking to Agnes while we ate mango, papaya, and banana. The fruit had been picked fresh that morning and gave my taste buds great cause for joy because the fruit was the juiciest and sweetest I had ever tasted.

A shower, a full stomach and warm sunshine made me feel on top of the world. I had no idea where we were in Nairobi, but it was beautiful. The huge leaves of several banana trees waved to us from across the street. Students, with arms full of books, were passing on the sidewalk in front of the hotel. They were dressed no differently than college students in the United States.

The smell of sweet flowers tickled my nose, and the gentle breeze kept us cool and comfortable. Unfortunately, it was time to go. We would be heading across Nairobi to Judy's house.

This was our first real look at the city of Nairobi. Leaving the Norfolk, we headed directly to the highway.

"What the hell is that?" I asked.

To the north of us was an area of Nairobi where houses were made of tree limbs, sticks, mud, and rusty, corrugated metal. There must have been thousands of these little shacks stacked one right next to the other.

This was Kibera, about one square mile where between eight hundred thousand and one million poverty-stricken Kenyans live. Kibera is not only the biggest slum in Africa; it is one of the largest in the world. In comparison, the city of San Francisco encompasses forty-seven square miles and has a population of about 730,000 residents. There are more than one hundred thousand orphaned children in Kibera—the vast majority as a result of AIDS.

We were too far away to see any details, but here was one-third of Nairobi's population living in conditions that were not fit enough for pigs. Sister Mary Theresa told us that we would not be visiting Kibera because it was a very violent place. Instead, later in the week, we would be visiting Korogocho. With nearly two hundred thousand residents, it is Nairobi's second largest slum.

Leaving the highway and after making a couple of left turns, we arrived at Judy's house. Her house was in a gated community, except that the gate was so rusty it no longer worked. A fat old black-and-white goat took residence on the roundabout in front of Judy's house. I joked with Tom wondering how much longer that goat would be alive considering the national dish of Kenya is *nyama choma*. Technically, nyama choma is any barbequed meat, but most commonly, it was barbequed goat.

Tom said that stealing a person's goat was considered more serious than stealing a person's wife. If caught, the goat thief could be stoned to death.

All the houses in the court had twelve-foot walls, with either barbed wire or shards of glass affixed to the top of the walls with concrete. The walls had large metal doors with locks and little peepholes. They were built like little fortresses. Nairobi is a poor country; more people are thieves than are employed in honest jobs, or at least, it seemed that way. One cannot take their possessions or their safety for granted.

Judy is Agnes's second oldest daughter. She was born during a "good time" in Agnes's life. During the trip, we met eight of Agnes's daughters. They all varied in size and strength. I have two children of my own, and it seemed apparent that life must have been tough for Agnes during the birth of her four middle children. You could form a dramatic curve if you plotted on a graph the relationship between the ages and physical appearances of Agnes's children. Her older and younger children are healthy big women. The four in the middle are small and appeared very frail.

Judy had graduated from college with a degree in public relations. She started working part-time after the birth of Diana, her five-year-old daughter. Right after they bought a house, Judy's husband, Peter, was sent by his company to work several hours away in Mombassa. He lives in an apartment in Mombassa during the week and commutes six hours each day on a bus to spend his weekends at home.

Considering the neighborhood, by our standards, Judy's little house was surprisingly nice. About eight hundred square feet with tile floors and an entertainment center stocked with all the modern electronics: twenty-five-inch television, stereo, and VCR.

As was customary in a Kenyan home, the guests are given the nicest seats in the house. In this case, it was a new yellow-and-brown sofa, with a paisley pattern. Across the back of the couch was a beautiful blanket, hand crocheted by Judy.

Little Diana was quite entertaining. We quickly nicknamed her Princess Diana because she was the ruler of the house. At five years old, she knew how to operate all the electronic gear. The princess did a good job driving Father Pat nuts by constantly changing the volume on the DVD player.

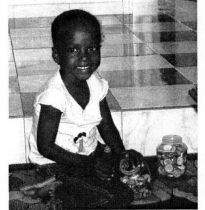

**Diana and her collection
of bottle caps.**

In the dining area, there was a sink. *What a weird place for a sink,* I thought. It was actually well placed to serve two purposes: the toilet was in a room next to it, and it was used to wash your hands before you ate. The Kenyans are very meticulous about washing their hands before eating. In restaurants, a waiter will pass a basin and pitcher of water around the table so one can wash their hands before eating.

Believe me, it is very odd feeling to come out of the bathroom and wash your hands in front of a room full of people.

Judy prepared a traditional Kenyan meal of white rice, brown beans, and a tortilla-like bread known as chapati, a thick gravylike broth with peas and carrots, and a stew with some kind of brown meat that was nearly impossible to chew. I was thinking I should run out to the front gate to see if that old goat was still out there.

Father Pat asked Agnes if the chewy meat was goat; she said no but did not tell us what kind of meat it was. Since we already ate it, we felt that our gastric juices would be better off if we did not know what the meat was. For some reason, though, I had this urge to lick my nuts and scratch behind my ear with my right leg.

With a full stomach and the unidentifiable meat stuck between our teeth, Father Pat and I found it hard to stay awake. The great thing about traveling with Father Pat is that when he is tired, the day's over. Tom drove us back to the Norfolk.

It was commute time in Nairobi. There were thousands and thousands of people on foot. There were poor women wearing colorful traditional Kenyan clothing, sitting on street corners, trying to sell a few mangos or papayas. The street salesmen were out, and Tom warned us to keep our windows rolled up.

"These guys will stick their hands in the car and steal your watch, sunglasses, or whatever they can get their hands on." Tom also added something that immediately grabbed my attention, "Be careful of young children coming up to the car, begging for money; they will try to extort money from you by smearing their feces on you." Needless to say, I never opened my window again. The salesmen were selling calendars, newspapers, cell phone accessories, tools, and just about anything else they could carry.

As we drove around a roundabout on our way to the hotel, we caught our first glimpse of the street girls. Tom told us that the three girls in question—no more than fourteen years old—lived on the roundabout and were washing their bright and colorful dresses in an old bucket to get ready for a night of selling their bodies for a few shillings. At a stoplight, filthy eight- and nine-year-old feces-packing boys ran among the cars, begging for money.

"This is why I wanted to come back," Father Pat said. "This is exactly what I saw in 2002. We need to find a way to help."

Chapter 3

Anthony and the Prostitute

What a joke! The first and, thank God, the last night at the Norfolk Hotel was over. Frogs, which sounded like they were the size of Godzilla, were croaking all night. The "luxurious beds," as quoted by the expensive-looking brochure, were luxurious when the hotel first opened in 1904. The only people to sleep on a harder surface would be the dead bodies on a marble slab at the city morgue.

Both our backs were stiff like overstarched dress shirts. It took all we had to stand up straight. A hot shower and a couple of Ibuprofen made life seem a little more bearable. After a quick breakfast, Tom, again dressed for golf, and Sister Christine arrived. We jumped into our Toyota Land Cruiser, and we were off.

Sister Christine is a little fireball. At four feet eight inches tall, everyone towered over her. Sister Christine's fire hydrant-shaped body was dressed neatly in a long bluish gray skirt, matching jacket, and white shirt. One thing for certain, you will never see Sister Christine without a smile.

Me, Sister Christine, Sister Mary Theresa, and Father Pat at the convent.

31

"How was your first night in Nairobi?" she asked.

"We are both looking forward to the convent," Father Pat explained. "One more night on that bed at the Norfolk and I would be crawling around on all fours." This would have been something worth staying one more night at the Norfolk to see now that I think of it.

Nairobi has all the elements of a modern city and is the commerce center of Kenya. Tourist hotels, night clubs, restaurants, and shopping malls are all over the city. My impression is that Nairobi was becoming very Western until the regime of Daniel Moi. Free trade and open commerce deteriorated during Moi's time as Kenya's president due to the perceived government corruption by the people of Kenya. Western influence came to a complete stop, leaving the citizens of Kenya stuck between the modern world and tribal history.

During our ride through Nairobi, we found thousands of people milling around, trying to catch a bus to work.

The city bus system is reliable but very expensive. Those who like to gamble with their lives or want a cheap ride will take a *matatu*. This is where life in Nairobi gets exciting. A matatu is a minivan. Usually, a minivan will hold seven to nine people. But if packed properly, one can cram over twenty people into one matatu.[6]

With the driver's favorite music playing as loud as possible, he understands only two speeds: stop and haulin' ass. While driving through Nairobi, we saw a matatu with its sliding door open and three people with their feet on the running board, their hands holding the luggage rack, and their asses hanging on to oncoming traffic. As we passed them, I counted twenty-one passengers. You haven't lived until you have flown seventy miles an hour down a potholed road with your ass hanging out of a matatu.

At a Stop sign, we purchased a copy of the *Daily Nation*, Kenya's national newspaper, from a street vendor. He was running in and out of traffic, dodging the cars like a pro football player.

On the front page was a photo of a man lying on the ground with a car tire around his neck. The paper told the story of a man who was accused of robbing his neighbor. The people in the neighborhood chased the guy down, beat the living hell out of him, put a tire around his neck, filled the tire with gasoline, and were ready to drop a match inside the tire when the police showed up. They broke up the crowd and took the man away.

Tom told us that "necklacing" was common during the Moi era. The police would usually look the other way unless they were bribed to do their job.

We took a right turn and headed up a one-lane, partially paved, partially rock, partially potholed road lined with tall green banana and mango trees. I had a sense

---

6   As of January 2005, the government of Kenya has declared that the number of passengers a matatu can carry cannot exceed the number of seats available. But they still haul ass.

of being in some bad B movie about dinosaurs and cavemen. Occasionally, I would catch a peek at a wooden shack with an old wrinkled woman, her head covered with an old faded scarf, cooking vegetables or meat on an open fire. The smoke from the fire wafted here and there with the warm, swirling jungle breeze.

Somewhere along the way, just like an old hound dog, Sister Mary Theresa, in her green Toyota Corolla, picked up our trail and followed us to our first stop of the day at the village of Mutuini[7] and St. Catherine of Labour Catholic Church and School. Her car was covered, like everything else, with a thick layer of sticky khaki-colored dust.

We pulled into a grassy area between the banana and mango trees and parked next to the gray-stone and wooden-roofed church of St. Catherine of Labour. Next to the church was the church hall, which was no more than a barn, that doubled as a meeting place for the nearby village of Kirinde and as a clinic where the locals would come seeking help from everything from a headache to AIDS.

We were greeted by the basketball-shaped and very black Sister Antoinette. She had been a nun for about twenty years and was very skilled working with the poor. She was from the slums, which helped her relate to the people at the clinic, as well as other parts of Nairobi for the archdiocese.

Sister Antoinette's short and round body made me wonder why all these nuns looked so well fed. The answer, I believe, is in all the starch they eat: rice, potatoes, beans, and thick fatty gravy.

We were also joined by Edward and Anthony. They were from the archdiocese of Nairobi's communications office. Their job was to film us during our trip. We were quickly introduced to them by Sister Mary Theresa, and I became immediately suspicious because I thought that we were going to be used for a propaganda and sympathy piece for the archdiocese.

I pulled Edward off to the side and asked him what the filming was for. He told me it was going to be a documentary of our visit. When he finally shipped it to us, it was just as we thought: a sympathy piece for the archdiocese.

Fresh from their Christmas holiday, about forty schoolchildren, ranging from five to twelve years old, were gathered outside of the schoolhouse, waiting for us. They were still dressed in their festive clothing. Their red sweaters, with pictures of Christmas trees and Santa Claus, made them look similar to the kids back home. Except for the humid and warm temperatures (and that it was the middle of January), the worn, once-colorful clothing brought Christmas back to me again.

Although primary education was declared free by the new government, children were still required to wear uniforms. The red sweaters and gray or blue slacks reminded me of the Catholic school that my kids barely survived. Not all the kids were in uniform, but none were turned away. Many of the families were so poor that

---

[7]   Mutuini is about twenty-five miles east of Nairobi

they could barely afford any clothing, let alone a uniform. Several of the children were wearing third or fourth hand-me-downs.

All the kids had short hair or had their hair in cornrows. We were told, after I asked, that the short hair and cornrows helped keep the lice away.

Sister Mary Theresa introduced us to the volunteers and teachers at the school. Their daily struggle, she told us, was getting the kids to come to school and to feed them. The kids were not receiving healthy, nutritious meals at home because most of their parents were sick with AIDS, drunk, or unemployed.

The kids looked beautiful and, much to our surprise, healthy. None of them spoke English, and they laughed when I said *jambo* and *habari*, which means hello and how are you in Swahili. Sister Christine told us that a few of the kids had never seen a white person before and certainly had never heard one speak Swahili.

Back home in American Canyon, we incorporate sign language into our Sunday Mass; while Father Pat was teaching the kids how to say "This is our daily bread" in sign language,

Father Pat and the children at St. Catherine Labour.

I had a chance to talk to Sister Antoinette.

She told me that 20 percent of the kids at the school were HIV-positive. Most were infected before birth by their parents and won't live past their teenage years. The kids live either in a shack along the road or in the village of Kirinde.[8]

Sister Antoinette pointed to a six-year-old girl named Christine and told me of her heart-tugging, sad story. (See front cover.)

"Do you see that girl over there, the one with her brother on her back?" she said. "Her father has died, and her mother lives in Kirinde. Her mother travels two

---

8   Kirinde is located two miles south of Mutuini.

hours to work and two hours back again. She walks the first hour to the bus, which takes her to the other side of Nairobi, where she cleans houses for a living. Christine is left in charge of her one-year-old brother. She carries him around wherever she goes. If Christine wants to come to school, she walks the two miles from Kirinde, with her brother on her back, goes to school, and then walks two miles home. She stays in the village, where neighbors look after her until her mother comes home well after dark. Her brother never leaves her back."

Father Pat called me over to the group of kids. We took turns blessing the kids by making the sign of the cross on their foreheads; we then asked the kids to bless us too. This would be the first and most likely the last time in their lives that they would bless a priest.

The tracing of the sign of the cross on a forehead is not new to the Catholic Church; but it is usually done when someone is receiving the sacraments of baptism, confirmation, or the anointing of the sick. Our parish believes that blessing someone in this manner should be done often and by everyone. It is an outward sign of claiming one for Christ.

The kids then sang a song in Swahili about how great God is in all the cities in Kenya. After more blessings and hugs, we headed to the church hall.

At the hall, eight mothers had come with their severely retarded children. Birth defects are much more common in Kenya than in developed countries because of malnutrition, the lack of medical care, and the heavy use of alcohol.

Most of these kids could not walk or talk. A few were able to make grunting noises, and others could not hold their heads up. The sad and guilt-filled eyes of the mothers gave away the pain they felt. Sister Antoinette explained to me that these mothers believed that it was their sins, which angered God, that caused their children to become crippled or retarded.

Having grown up around doctors and nurses, I could tell that Sister Antoinette was talking to me with a clinical detachment that is usually common in the medical profession. It appeared to be a way for her to protect herself from the daily pain and drama of the people she served.

Sister Mary Theresa called Father Pat to a grassy area between the hall and the church. She introduced him to a little boy named Anthony. He was not quite two years old. Little Anthony had that look of wonderment, which I have seen so many times on the faces of two-year-olds back home. He was a damn cute little kid.

Sister Mary Theresa told us that Anthony was a typical child from Kirinde. He looked healthy because he was being fed by the church. But Anthony had HIV. His mother was HIV-positive when Anthony was conceived. No one knew who Anthony's father was. Soon Anthony's mother will be dead, and he will be orphaned with no one having the responsibility to give him his medicine.

"He will have a short life, but we will try and make it a happy one," Sister Mary Theresa said.

The thought of Anthony being orphaned and having to live in the streets angered and frustrated Father Pat. But holding little Anthony in his arms transformed his emotions from anger to sympathy and sadness. Father Pat has always had a soft spot for kids. We were only a couple of days into our trip, and already, he was experiencing what he later described as the defining moment of his trip.

He wanted so desperately to connect with little Anthony. He did the only thing he could. He held little Anthony's egg-shaped head close to his cheek and said, "This is my brother." He looked deeply into Anthony's bright black eyes; and with a tear streaming down his cheek, Father Pat proclaimed for all of us around him to hear, "Anthony, you are my brother."

Realizing that he was crying, Father **Father Pat and HIV-positive Anthony.**
Pat turned away from the brilliant, life-giving sunshine; set Anthony back down on the ground; and walked away from us to regain his composure.

"Holding Anthony in my arms and hearing his story touched me so deeply that there was nothing else I could do but cry," Father Pat later explained.

It was time to head down the road to the village of Kirinde. Sister Antoinette called all the children up to the clinic, and they shook our hands before we got back into the Land Cruiser.

Turning right on the dusty road, I pulled out a bottle of instant hand sanitizer and asked Father Pat if he thought I would be offending anyone if I used some of it. Tom, our driver, heard me and said, "Hell no. Let me have some of that when you are done." What a relief that was. After touching all those children and adults, whom I am sure have not bathed in quite some time, well, I wanted to take a bath in the stuff.

Kirinde appeared to be a ghost town; pulling into the center of the town, we saw no one. The village was built from discarded wood, tree limbs, and rusty metal. There were two or three units in each building, giving the inhabitants a space less than the size of a master bathroom in a modern house back home. No electricity, plumbing, or running water were available either.

It was already getting hot, and the high clouds were making it quite humid. The foul smell of sewage mixed with burning trash made us all want to get back in the car.

The sisters were taking us to see Naomi, an ex-prostitute who contracted AIDS about two years ago; but a crazy man, named Don, appeared from nowhere and was hell-bent on attacking us. His brown double-knit slacks were dirty and full of holes, and his shirt was yellowed with age. Don looked and acted like he was on a two-month bender. He would have made a great poster boy for Alcoholics Anonymous.

Kenyans love to make their own liquor. We were told by Edward that the homemade brew, called *chang'a*, had killed 130 people and sent another 500 to the hospital last November. The recipe for chang'a includes fermented marijuana branches, battery acid, and methanol. With no jobs and people dying of AIDS all around you, there is not much else to do but make your own hooch and get drunk.

Crazy Don charged at us, waving his arms and screaming in Swahili at the top of his lungs. He was spilling the contents of a clay mug all over himself. If the situation was not serious, I would have thought it quite humorous. Don definitely livened up the day.

I was thinking, *What the hell; here is Father Pat, sixty-three years old, me, and a bunch of old nuns. There was no way I was going to fight Don.* I turned to survey the scene and formulated my options. Father Pat had nicely positioned himself so Sister Mary Theresa was between him and Don. Then, just like the cavalry, Edward, the cameraman, appeared out of nowhere; injected his six-feet-one, 210-pound frame right in front of Don; and, just like the lion tamer who worked with the big African cats, distracted him until we were out of sight.

Don, I'm sure, visited his share of prostitutes in his day as it was quite common for the men of these small villages to do; but he was angry that we were going to visit Naomi, the ex-prostitute. When I was told this by Sister Antoinette, I wondered how he knew that we were visiting her. Sister Antoinette told me that she is a frequent visitor of Naomi and that she brings her food and clothing.

We headed down a narrow dirt alley being careful to walk in the middle of the path. If you veered to one side or another, you would hit your forehead on the rusty metal roof that hung down into the walkway.

We finally reached the end of the alley where Naomi lived. The smell of marijuana floated across our path. Just beyond where we were standing, two men had set a fire to clear some brush on a piece of land. Father Pat whispered in my ear, asking me if I had the munchies.

Sister Mary Theresa, Naomi, and Antoinette.

Sister Antoinette went into Naomi's shack and, after a few minutes, brought out a chair for Naomi to sit on; and then Naomi came out too.

There was no doubt that Naomi was sick. Her skin was just hanging from her bones. Her helpless-looking eyes were sunken so deep into her head that it looked painful for her to blink. The pain and guilt in her dull eyes were evident. I was surprised to see her wearing a hand-knit sweater and a long blue-and-gold skirt. It must have been eighty-five degrees outside, but Naomi was cold.

Naomi only spoke Swahili, so Sister Antoinette translated for us. Naomi had to take a break after each sentence because she was so weak. We were held spellbound by Sister Antoinette's translation: Since the age of fifteen, Naomi was a very popular girl. She lived in a village north of Nairobi. Her family was not exactly poor, but all of her seven brothers and sisters had to work to keep food on the table.

Naomi was the oldest child and had to work and take care of her siblings while her parents worked long hours in Nairobi. She was desperate for attention and found comfort by becoming intimate with several of the village boys. When her father lost his job, she started charging for sex. It helped keep food on the table, but the odds finally caught up to her; and she contracted HIV. She knew that she was HIV-positive for quite sometime but kept having sex because she needed the money. Naomi had no idea how many others she infected.

When she could no longer hide her illness, she was cast aside and sent away by her family. Sister Antoinette had become her best friend. When Naomi first came to Kirinde, she was frequently beaten by some of the men of the village because she would not have sex with them. Then when they found out she was HIV-positive, they stopped wanting sex but beat her all the same.

We took a look inside of Naomi's house. It was a five-by-six-foot room with a dirty mattress on the floor. She had a chair and washbasin against the wall. That five-by-six-foot room has been Naomi's only existence for the last year. She is now too weak to venture much farther than the doorway of her shack.

Father Pat blessed her, and she seemed very grateful. As he prayed with her, I put my hand on her left shoulder and gently rubbed it. Naomi responded the same way a dog does when you scratch behind its ears. She leaned into my hand, in a way that was telling me that she missed human physical contact.

As we weaved our way back to the main road, we passed by Don's shack, but Don was no longer interested in us. He had passed out, lying face down, in the dirt by his campfire.

By the time we got back to the Land Cruiser, a large group of dusty kids had gathered around it. They knew that Sister Antoinette was there, and they wanted to see her. She was quite popular with the kids because a couple of afternoons a week, she would gather them around and read to them. Today, there would be no stories, but Sister Antoinette introduced us to all the kids and to some of their mothers too.

I could envision a time when Kirinde was a poor but thriving community, with its own school and the inhabitants had their own sense of purpose. Today there were about 150 people living there, and it was estimated that 80 of them were HIV-positive or had full-blown AIDS. It was a village waiting to die.

By contrast, Kirinde presented a totally different picture than what we saw at the school in Mutuini. At the school, being away from the illness and despair, we saw bright, happy children, who had no worries and seemed to have a purpose in life. It was difficult to resist the urge to round up all the kids and take them home with us.

Back in the Land Cruiser, we once again bathed in hand sanitizer. I was feeling hungry but did not feel like eating. Sister Mary Theresa packed plenty of bananas and water for us. Today would be my first encounter with her banana fanaticism.

I expected more from a banana fresh from the tree, but they did not taste much different than the bananas from the supermarket back home. Sister Mary Theresa was a banana freak. She forced us to eat so many bananas during our visit that, after I arrived back home, it took my system two weeks to recover.

I never asked Sister Mary Theresa why she was so enamored with bananas. Was it their shape? Did it remind her of an old boyfriend? Who the hell knows, but Father Pat and I spent the rest of the trip teasing her about her love of the banana. The best thing about it was she never knew we were teasing her.

Tom sped along the road, dodging stray goats and cows. They seemed to be walking by themselves; there was no shepherd to be found.

Father Pat and I were ready to see something positive, and our stop at Rescue Data Center (RDC) was just what we needed.

The RDC is a volunteer center. The workers go to the streets, talk to the teenage mothers, and invite them to the center for a warm meal. They get to know the girls and their issues. They gain the confidence of these street girls by empathizing with their problems. The workers make sure that the street girls know there is a place where they are welcome, respected, and will be given an opportunity to put some meaning into their lives.

Tom pulled the Land Cruiser in front of the RDC, swerving to miss the biggest pothole I had ever seen. It looked like a moon crater. Tom said that the street had been sinking for about six months, and the government had yet to fix it.

The entrance to the center was well hidden by a huge tree. The cinder block front looked like it was painted with graffiti, but upon closer inspection, it was painted by many of the kids who stayed there. The colorful building stood out like a sore thumb, just about like Father Pat and I did in Nairobi.

The building had a rectangular shape and took up about half a city block. In the center was a courtyard with toys for the kids to play with. The building had various doors opening into the courtyard. Each door was colorfully painted, which was in stark contrast to the dirty streets outside. The rooms around the courtyard contained a kitchen, dining room, classrooms, a dispensary, and living quarters.

To survive the streets of Nairobi is to find a way to get off them. Hunger, crime, rape, drugs, murder, and mob rule is the daily life that the street people face. The average woman in Kenya does not enjoy the same benefits as men. Girls on the streets are looked upon as possessions to be used and then discarded.

If one is unskilled and lives on the streets, how does one feed their children? The girls turn to prostitution. This way, they are able to provide a meal for their kids; but at some point, they will contract HIV, die, and leave their kids to live on the streets to follow the same destructive pattern. The cycle is vicious, violent, deadly, and seemingly never ending.

We arrived at the center just in time for the kids to have lunch. The girls between the ages of three and six were grouped around small picnic tables. Because they knew that we were coming for a visit, the girls were wearing their best dresses. The bright-colored dresses of blue, green, and yellow with lace collars were made by their teenage mothers.

Girls eating lunch at the Rescue Data Center.

The girls were hungry; and they attacked their rice and bean bowls with their bare hands, scooping copious amounts of the brown-and-white-colored contents of their plastic Tupperware bowls into their happy mouths.

Sister Mary Theresa introduced us to Diana, who stood five feet six, very slender, and dressed in a red blazer and a blue dress. She had been the director of the center for five years. Her hair, combed straight and parted on the right, gave her the look of a Wall Street businesswoman. She spoke perfect English, and quite frankly, she was a knockout. She told us more about the center.

"The center was started five years ago," Diana said. "I have been here since the beginning. Many of the girls who come here see this place as their last hope. Life on the streets is very dangerous. Most of the girls here have been beaten and raped. We provide counseling to help them get over the trauma. About 25 percent of the girls that come here are HIV-positive. We do our best to contact their parents. Some of the girls want to go home. Others would rather stay here."

She continued, "Their children are fed and taught in our schools. Our schools are designed to get the children up to the grade level that they should be. We then enroll them in Catholic or public schools. We take all girls into the center: Catholic, Protestant, and Muslim; it does not matter."

Diana then took us to meet Amy, who worked in the dispensary as the resident health care worker. The dispensary had two beds for the sick kids and mothers. There were also several closets, well stocked with medicine and first-aid supplies. Amy was not trained to be a doctor or a nurse but applied common sense to her diagnosis.

Amy was quite proud of her work and had become proficient in treating some of the common ailments. The extremely sick patients are taken by taxi to the hospital in Nairobi. If the women or children become seriously ill with AIDS, they are moved to a care home run by the diocese.

It was time to head back to the convent. Tom drove us away from the center of the city to the neighborhood where most of the foreign ambassadors lived. We found ourselves on well-paved streets lined with large palm trees.

High walls and barbed wire guarded the beautiful old homes. Many of the houses had armed guards posted at the front gate. Tom made a quick turn into the driveway of the convent.

He whispered to us that the guard was a Maasai.

"How can you tell?" Father Pat queried.

"First, you can tell by the shape of his head: flat forehead and a long-shaped head. Plus, he has that huge hole in his earlobe for an earring," Tom said.

I was curious and asked, "Do tribes discriminate against each other?"

"Unfortunately, they do," he said. "The Kikuyu, which I am, have been the dominate tribe in Nairobi since it became a city. Things are better now; but there was a time that if you were not Kikuyu, you could not get a job."

The Maasai are one of the last traditional tribes of Kenya. It was not uncommon to see them wrapped in their traditional four-feet-wide colorful blanket with lots of necklaces and huge earrings. The women are typically clothed only from the waist down.

They are a nomadic tribe, wandering the countryside with their herds of cattle. The tribal Maasai do not eat meat or vegetables or sell or kill their cows. They live off the blood and milk of their cows. They are polygamous, leaving their wives in various towns as they roam around the country, tending to their cattle.

Chapter 4

Korogocho

The convent looked like a safe-enough place. We did get a chuckle from the security measures on top of the fence. It was just like Judy's house, broken bottles and shards of glass attached to the top of the fence with concrete. It looked effective; I would not try to climb it.

The convent grounds were very well kept. The lawns were kept nice and short by two goats: an all-white female and a black-and-white male. The goats had the run of the place. Previously, there were three goats until last April when one was served as the main course at Easter.

Tom parked the Land Cruiser and helped us with our luggage. The J. J. McCarthy convent sat on a hillside and was constructed from bricks and cinder blocks. The grounds were quite spacious. Being inside the walls gave us a sense of security and a surreal feeling that we were far removed from the crime and sickness of Nairobi.

Sister Mary Theresa said that she would be back at 6:00 p.m. to take us to dinner.

"Damn," said Father Pat. He was ready to unpack, relax, and turn in early.

I let Father Pat choose his room first, but it really didn't matter because both rooms were exactly the same: Futon-style beds, a desk, a chair, and a closet. Each room had a picture of the Virgin Mary above the bed. I considered removing the picture because it made me feel a little uncomfortable, but I figured that maybe she would protect me from being bitten by malaria-carrying mosquitoes.

The common area that connected the rooms was a little institutional for me. The linoleum floors, faded white walls, and worn chairs reminded me of a scene from *One Flew Over the Cuckoo's Nest*.

Before unpacking, I stepped outside and took a deep breath. The air was surprisingly fresh, considering there are no emission controls on the cars and buses. We must have been far enough away from the main roads to avoid the smell of burning oil. The air was still a little sticky from the humidity, but it was comfortable.

"I smell chicken," I said to Father Pat. The nuns were preparing dinner for the guests that were staying at the convent.

Standing out on the walkway, Father Pat mentioned that we needed to have Tom stop at the liquor store for us tomorrow. Although the convent rules prohibited alcohol on the premises, we both knew that our stay would be much more enjoyable ending the day with a cocktail. Before we could finish our conversation, we heard a commotion down the hall. Our neighbors had arrived.

We met Donna, Pastor Dan, and his wife, Rene. Donna was a frequent visitor to Kenya. She was not Catholic, but because of her work with the poor and abandoned, the sisters always found her a place to stay. Pastor Dan and his wife, Rene, were from Indiana. Dan was the pastor of his own Baptist Church and came to Kenya at the invitation of Donna. It was evident that Pastor Dan was having a bad day.

Father Pat started the conversation, "So, Dan, you look tired."

"Today is our last day in Kenya, and it has been a very long one. Have you been to the slums?"

"We are going to Korogocho tomorrow," Father Pat said.

Dan was black, about fifty years old, five feet ten, had a jolly big round face, and was built like a tank. He carried his extra forty-or-so pounds very well. Dan said that he traveled to Kenya to try and feel some connectedness to Africans. He wanted to tell us about his experience in Korogocho, but he broke down and started to cry, which caught Father Pat and I by surprise.

"I have never seen anything like that before," Dan said after he caught his breath. "I don't understand how people can live that way. They told me what to expect before we got there, but you can't prepare yourself for that."

Father Pat and I wanted to ask Dan a few questions because we were going there in the morning. I could tell that Dan was a little embarrassed by his breakdown, and he quickly retreated to his room.

Dan's reaction should have caused me alarm, but it energized me; and I was more than eager for our next day's adventure.

It was almost time for Sister Mary Theresa to pick us up for dinner, so we headed out to the courtyard. The late afternoon was relaxing. It was still quite warm, but a slight breeze kept us comfortable.

Father Pat lit a cigarette and asked me what I thought of Dan breaking down.

"He said that he had been here for ten days and was looking for some connection with the Africans. Sometimes people look into the eyes of the suffering and see themselves," I said.

I thought that my observation and comment was quite profound, but Father Pat started laughing. I barely noticed that the black-and-white goat has snuck up on me and was enjoying nibbling on my shirt. Father Pat's laugh scared him away.

Before we could finish our conversation, Sister Mary Theresa arrived and drove us to dinner.

Sister took us to the Spur restaurant located at the Nairobi Holiday Inn. The restaurant did their best to look like the Old West. Waiters were dressed as cowpokes, and the waitresses were dressed like Ms. Kitty on *Gunsmoke*, with barmaid outfits typical of the Old West. The menu featured cowboy steak, cow burgers, and Indian sodas.

Father Pat and I had a cold Tusker beer and a big steak. The last time we had eaten, besides some almonds back at the convent, was breakfast.

About halfway through dinner, Sister Mary Theresa finished a glass of wine and started talking wildly about her childhood and how she wanted to be a police officer but became a nun instead. The funny thing was we could not understand her because she was slurring her words and was mixing altogether Swahili, English, and her native Kikuyu dialect. Sister Christine, who was having dinner with us, just rolled her eyes and translated for us. I was thinking, *Great! We are going to be driven back to the convent by a drunken nun.*

The drive back was interesting. The Daytona 500 was the first thing that came to mind. Traveling on one roundabout, I was sure we would tip onto two wheels. Fortunately, there were not many people on the streets after dark; so when Sister Mary Theresa blew right through a Stop sign, we thankfully didn't hit anyone.

Father Pat and I said quick good nights, and we made a pact right there with each other; we would not let Sister Mary Theresa drink again, at least as long as we were around.

The next morning, Tom arrived promptly at 9:00 a.m., and we were on our way to Korogocho.

Nairobi was alive. Commuters, in cars and on foot, filled the streets. The number of people downtown reminded me of any weekday in New York City. Except the cabs were matatus with passengers hanging from luggage racks and everyone as far as the eye could see had black skin.

On one street corner, we saw a man with a six-foot air tank, offering drivers a chance to fill their tires for a few shillings. On another corner, a butcher shop featured a half cow and a half goat hanging in its window. The building was a metal shack with no air-conditioning or refrigeration. I wondered how the meat stayed fresh enough to eat.

We picked up a copy of the *Daily Nation* from a street vender. The front page featured a feud between President Mwai Kibaki's two wives. Although it is common and accepted for Kenyans to have more than one wife, Kibaki is Catholic, and polygamy is forbidden in the church. However, the bishops and priests have turned the other cheek because Kibaki promised, if elected, to root out government corruption and put people back to work.

The task ahead of him is daunting. Kibaki had been part of Kenyan politics before the split with Great Britain and had run against Daniel Moi three previous times. But 2002 was a magic year for the seventy-one-year-old president. Forging an alliance with the Liberal Democratic Party, he formed the National Rainbow Coalition, also known as NARC. With the backing of the new coalition, Kibaki won the election with 63 percent of the vote.

The ride to Korogocho surprised me because it was so short. We pulled into the parking lot of the Holy Trinity Catholic Church located in Kairobangi, the town neighboring Korogocho.

While we waited for our escort, I wandered into the church. The worship space was very large. A priest, who was straightening up the pews, told me that five thousand people attend in five masses on Sundays.

Hand-painted Bible scenes adorned the walls around the inside. There was a black Moses; a scene of the Last Supper, where all the disciples were black; and a scene of the Nativity, in which Mary, Joseph, and Jesus were black. I chuckled because I never realized until that moment that for the Bible to speak to you, you have to relate to it. What better way than seeing the people of the Bible as your own race?

"Mike! Mike! Come on, Mike," Sister Mary Theresa called for me.

I have a bad habit of wandering off without telling anyone. I could tell, by the tone of her voice, that Sister Mary Theresa was a little annoyed with me. I was holding up the group.

Sister Mary Theresa introduced us to one of the most amazing women I had ever met. Her name was Sister Jill. At first, she came off as a crusty old Irish nun. Her sun-baked and wrinkly white face gave the impression that she was much older than her actual fifty years; but after spending a few minutes with her, I quickly saw a woman whose love and compassion were contagious.

I nearly fell over when she said that she had been working in Korogocho for seventeen years. She came to Korogocho, directly from Ireland, seventeen years ago to do six months of missionary work; except for a short vacation from time to time, she has never left.

Sister Jill is energetic, positive, and full of energy. From all the death and despair she had seen over the years, I could not understand how she could continue to find beauty in this.

Korogocho is Nairobi's second largest slum. Although there is no official census, because the previous administration neglected the entire settlement, it is estimated that there is somewhere between 170,000 and 200,000 people living there.

By 1986, when she came to Korogocho, HIV and AIDS were already an epidemic. But it was not understood how it was transmitted. Back then, catching AIDS was a quick death sentence.

We were all crammed into Sister Jill's small office when her assistant came in to ask for money to go to Nairobi to purchase medical supplies. She gave the woman money from her own wallet.

"Are you paying for that yourself?" I needed to know.

"Only until tomorrow. That is when we should receive some funds from the Catholic Church in Germany. We are out of money right now."

The church in Germany and the Netherlands have adopted Korogocho and contribute much-needed money each month to Sister Jill so she can purchase medical supplies for her patients.

Several years ago, Sister Jill set up a clinic in the heart of the slums. People came to the clinic on a volunteer basis to be tested for HIV and to receive medications to help them survive. Sister Jill explained to us that the medications that are used to treat HIV in Western countries are dangerous to the patients in Korogocho.

"The people here are so malnourished, and the meds are so powerful that they make the patients very sick and could end up killing them."

Sister Jill explained to us that they have found other means to help with secondary infections: folic acid cures thrush, and vitamin B6 is used to treat nervous system disorders.

"So, Sister," I asked, "what you are doing here is helping people die comfortably."

"We are helping them die with dignity," she corrected me. "Every human life deserves that."

Sister Jill had trained twenty volunteers to help her in Korogocho. Ten of the volunteers keep medical records and organize the medicine. They are the pharmacists.

The other ten are trained to be nurses. They help administer the meds and take general care of the patients. These people are all volunteers, and three of the ten are HIV-positive themselves. These HIV nurses know that someday they will be on the other side receiving care from Sister Jill's nurses.

Sister Jill revealed to us that every week in Korogocho, five people die from AIDS and ten new cases of HIV are diagnosed. I wanted to know what they were doing to educate people to keep them from becoming infected. Sister Jill said that her group has been distributing information person to person and that the new government has a huge ad campaign to educate the people. But it is a very difficult and slow process.

"You have to first gain their trust and then get them to unlearn the myths associated with the disease. Then they will listen to you. But it's hard work and very time-consuming to build that trust," she said.

Suddenly, there was quite a bit of commotion outside of Sister Jill's office. A woman was wheeled into the courtyard on a padded gurney. This gurney was designed to shuttle patients between the clinic and the slums. It had two large wheels in the back and a long round handle used for someone to pull the cart. It reminded me somewhat of a cart you would see a horse pull.

Sister Jill explained to us that if someone was too sick to be helped at the clinic, they would be put on one of these mobile gurneys and wheeled to the church compound. They are then taken to the church hall and hooked up to an IV to rehydrate them and to give them some rest. The hall was filled with people.

I commented to Sister Jill that it reminded me of a mobile army hospital. She said that that was a good analogy as most of the time she feels that they are at war with AIDS.

We were ready to drive into Korogocho. Sister Jill told us to stay close to her and to leave cameras, watches, etc., in the car; otherwise, someone would mug us. We then followed Sister Jill in our vehicle.

Entering the slums of Korogocho was like going to a shopping mall and safari all at once. The animals lurked around every corner, waiting to pounce on their unsuspecting prey. The animals, of course, were the thieves of Korogocho.

The cleaner shops with better merchandise—better, of course, being relative— were at the entrance to the slums. The brave souls from the surrounding areas would venture to these shops. It was the cheap prices that made it worth their while to risk being mugged.

The shops, like the entire slum, were built from tree branches, mud, chicken wire, palm leaves, and rusty metal. The three shops we saw had Western clothing, Nike and Adidas sneakers, soccer jerseys from the English Premier League teams, and other items that you would normally find at a sportswear shop at home. The difference was that the items were used, stolen, or being sold on consignment.

The skin of the people we saw wasn't black but looked like chocolate milk because of dust that covered their faces, arms, and legs. Many wore clothing not worthy by Salvation Army standards. Dirty shirts, sweatshirts with holes worn in the elbows, and tattered blue jeans were the fashion of the day. The people all looked like Lon Chaney's Frankenstein: blank expressions on their faces, wandering about without purpose. There was no doubt about it—this was a dangerous place.

Beyond the shops came the restaurants all advertising the best nyama choma, barbequed goat, in Korogocho, and all three of the restaurants had skinned headless goats hanging in their windows. I know I mentioned it before, but how the hell does that meat stay fresh? At home, we would never purchase meat hanging in a hot, dusty window like that.

It was difficult driving because the dirt roads were narrow, and there were people everywhere. Tom was skilled at dodging the people, the potholes, and the goats.

After what seemed like hours—it was actually about twenty minutes—we arrived at our destination: Sister Jill's clinic in the heart of Korogocho. We parked the cars and walked several hundred feet to the entrance.

The odor of burning old meat filled the air: it was a nasty smell, and it burned my nostrils. It was lunchtime for the locals, and some people were selling fruit and barbequed meat. Upon entering the slums, we were definitely being watched. It felt like we were under a microscope. All eyes were following our every move.

Sister Jill reminded us to stay close to her and walk in the middle of the street. Open drainage ditches, which were cut in a willy-nilly way, and plastic shopping bags being tended to by thousands of flies were the main attractions.

The drainage ditches were dry, but Sister Jill told us that the bags were filled with human excrement. It was quite unnecessary for her to tell us what was in the bags. The smell gave away its contents.

"Oh great," Father Pat whispered to me, "bags of shit."

"Toilets are communal and privately owned. The owners charge a few shillings to use them. During the night, when it's cold or the people don't have any money, they use the bags as their toilets and then throw the bags into the street." Sister continued, "These are the flying toilets of Kenya."

A little girl about three years old, wearing a tattered pink-and-white dress, seemed fascinated with Father Pat's gorilla-like hairy arms; she came running at him and, while petting his arms, said, "Jambo mzungu. Jambo mzungu."

Everyone but Father Pat and I started laughing because we were the only ones who did not understand Swahili.

"What is she saying?" asked Father Pat.

"Hello, white man. Hello, white man," Sister Mary Theresa translated for us. Then we both joined in the laughter.

Sister Jill led us down a narrow alley and through a short and narrow doorway. There was a drainage ditch cut down the center of the alley; we were all careful not to step in it. Sister Jill's volunteer pharmacists and nurses worked in a twenty-by-twenty-foot room. Each nurse was paired with a pharmacist.

AIDS clinic in Korogocho.

The workers stopped when we walked in. Sister Jill introduced us to everyone, but I'll be damned if I could remember any of their names.

In a small room next to the clinic was Jon. He was so thin that a light breeze would have blown him over. Jon was lying on a table with an IV of glucose stuck in his left arm.

Sister Jill explained, "Many of the AIDS patients get diarrhea and become dehydrated. We used to put them in a taxi and send them to the hospital, but the wait was so long at the hospital and the taxi ride so costly that we have taught ourselves how to administer an IV."

Jon was dreadfully weak and could hardly hold his head up. One thing was common among the sick: they craved human touch. I held Jon's hand, and he gripped it as hard as he could and didn't let go until it was time for us to go. We all prayed over him. Jon managed a smile as we were leaving.

"What will happen to him?" I asked Sister Jill.

"He will be rehydrated and go home."

Father Pat wanted to know and asked, "How much longer will he live?"

"Less than six months, I would imagine," Sister Jill sadly told us.

While we headed back to the street, the bright sunlight was blinding and made it difficult to make sure we were not going to step in a trench or the remains of a flying toilet.

We next visited Carol, who was in charge of HIV testing and counseling. Carol's big brown eyes and comforting smile made you feel right at home. She was about thirty-five years old but already had that grandmotherly way about her, someone that could hold your hand and make your pain go away.

Her job was to administer the blood tests, which were then sent to a lab at a hospital in Nairobi.

Carol, after shaking our hands, explained that her job was to counsel the patients and help them understand their blood tests.

"Some days are better than others. My patients know that a positive HIV test is a death sentence. We try to keep the information as private as possible, so they won't be treated poorly by the community."

I was surprised that, with these people living in squalid conditions and with each day bringing such danger and hunger, the formality of privacy was still carried out with the AIDS patients.

Carol explained that the dignity of the person must be protected first and foremost.

"Quite frankly, it is no one's business if a person tests positive or not," she said.

I pressed further, "In this environment, wouldn't it be a benefit that people knew who was HIV-positive?"

Carol was showing great patience with my questioning. "In a perfect, caring world, that might be true; but in a society where people still don't understand how HIV is transmitted and many believe that HIV is some kind of punishment, a person's HIV status could get them killed before the disease can take their life."

Although Carol talked about how privacy was so important, we could hear a woman in the next room crying.

"What's up with the crying?" Father Pat asked.

"She is one of the lucky ones. Before I came out to meet all of you, I told her the results of her HIV test. She tested negative."

Father Pat asked if he could bless her. Carol checked with the woman and then let Father Pat into the next room.

Sister Jill answered my question before I was able to ask it. She explained to me that this was a typical day at the clinic. There were tears shed all day long, some in joy and some in sadness.

"Today," Sister Jill said, "was a good day."

While we waited for Father Pat to come back, I harkened back to Pastor Dan and how he broke down. Seeing the pending death on Jon's face, the flying toilets, and the dusty, dirty people wandering around without any purpose, I now understood the depth of his sorrow.

I had a question that had been bothering me for the last hour or so. "Sister Jill, how do you do this day in and day out? Every single day, you see sickness and death. How do you keep your strength? How do you keep your sanity?"

Her answer was quite typical of everyone I asked that question to during the trip.

"I get my strength from the people I serve. Every day I see sick and dying people who express their love for God, who keep going, who keep the faith. They make do with what they have, and no matter how sick they are, they always want to help someone else." Her answer choked me up.

Father Pat and I quietly made our way back to the car. We stopped for a few minutes to watch a group of teenagers playing soccer on a makeshift field. There were large rocks set up as goals and a ball made from old plastic grocery bags and cloth all tied together. I vowed right there that when I returned, I would bring soccer balls with me.

It took even longer to get out of Korogocho than going in. There were masses of people walking aimlessly down the street, oblivious that there were cars behind them. I was trying to take photos through the Land Cruiser's windows. It was difficult because there were men who appeared to be drunk or on drugs, who kept coming up and peering inside the windows. It made me feel like I was at the zoo. But I was the one in the cage.

Watching all these sick, drugged, and drunk people made for a sad ending to an exceedingly emotional day. You could see that these people had lost hope. They had empty expressions, trying to get through the day—a day that ran right into the next day and into the next, bringing with it a never-ending cycle of hopelessness and despair. We saw the same people sitting by open fires, cooking meat and selling fruit. I noticed a bar with a Tusker sign across the doorway. I wondered what it would be like to go in and have a beer.

I asked Father Pat how it went with the women he went to bless.

"She did not think I was a priest because of my ponytail and street clothes. Carol assured her I was, and then she wanted to do a confession. I blessed her; she blessed me; and that was it."

I sure wanted to know what she confessed. I bet it was pretty interesting, but being a priest, Father Pat was held under the "seal of confession." This means that no matter what the person confesses, the priest cannot talk about it to anyone. It remains between the priest, God, and the confessor.

Tom had a memory like a steel trap. He never forgot a request we had the entire time we were there. Out of Korogocho and on the road back to Nairobi, he pulled off at a shopping mall.

"You wanted to purchase some medicine before you headed back the convent, right?" Tom asked.

Ah yes, a fifth of Beefeater gin and a fifth of Johnny Walker. It was just what the doctor ordered after our day in the slums of Korogocho.

Chapter 5

Thika

Back at the convent, we had about an hour or so before dinner, which gave us a chance to relax and reflect on the day. Father Pat's well-practiced ritual of having a cocktail before dinner was somewhat new to me but has since become favorite a ritual of mine too.

I brought out a couple of chairs, and we sat under the covered walkway between our wing and the main building. The walkway had a view of the conference rooms and a patch of grass that was in desperate need of water. At the end of the walkway sat a five-hundred-gallon water container. It was well placed to collect water from the metal roof of the main house.

After our second drink, we began to talk about how Korogocho had to be the bottom of the barrel but that we were also inspired to have seen its positive side too. We saw sick people being tended to with warmth and care. We saw hope in some eyes, and we saw the smiles and happiness on the faces of the children, too small to understand that they lived in the slums.

Sister Jill had told us that Korogocho is a much different place at night. She had told us stories of gangs terrorizing the residents, robbing what few possessions they had, and about the raping of the young girls, with the assumption that the younger girls did not have AIDS. The hunt for virgins went on night after night with no help from the police.

Sister Jill did explain to us that crime was way down because some representatives from the new government came in and promised to help and so far had delivered fresh water, food, and the opportunities for some of the kids to go to school. But besides the promises of the government to help the souls in the slums, no help has been given to protect its citizens.

We have heard the sisters and many of the other people we have met talk about how the new government was going to help them. All of this discussion upset me because if the citizens of Nairobi sat around waiting for the government to help them, they would have a very long wait. The task of putting the pieces back together in Kenya would be monumental. It would take a superman to solve all the problems. Mwai Kibaki is known as a gentleman politician and someone who is true to his word, but the problems are huge and complex.

Taking all I have read about Kenya into consideration and all that I have seen so far, it seemed to me that the solution resides in education. Get the kids to the schools and help them build a better future. This process has already started. Right after President Kibaki took office, he opened up the primary grades (K-8) to all children, abolishing the prohibitive fees that have been charged for so many years.

What had impressed Father Pat and me so far was that the programs put together by Sister Mary Theresa and the Archdiocese of Nairobi were not handout programs; they were designed to help train the poor and the abandoned children to be self-sufficient.

*   *   *

The next morning, breakfast consisted of eggs; sausage of unknown ingredients; a bologna-like lunchmeat; and an abundance of fresh bananas, papayas, and mangos. This was a great way to start the day.

Kenyan tea, in my opinion, is the best in the world; but what makes me chuckle is the manner in which they drink it. They drink it British style: half hot water, half hot milk. The milk we were drinking was right from the cow, which was tearing up my stomach. After a couple of days, I could not drink it anymore. So this day, I asked for my tea to be black.

"Just black? No milk?" Sister Mary Theresa and Sister Christine asked nearly in unison. "But THIS is how we drink our tea in Kenya."

"But this is not how I like my tea." Watching both the sisters' faces very closely, I continued, "I like my tea like I like my women." The questioning expressions from the sisters let me know that I had them. "I like my tea like I like my women," I repeated and added, "Hot, black, and strong!"

Sister Christine laughed so hard that I thought I saw the tea she was drinking come out of her nose. I don't think Sister Mary Theresa got it because she still insisted that I take milk in my tea.

To this day, when I receive correspondence from Sister Christine, she concludes by asking me how I am enjoying my "hot black tea."

Sister Mary Theresa was very excited and quite anxious to show us her hometown of Thika. She wanted to give us a feel of what it was like growing up on a tea farm and how things were so much better when she was a child. While Sister Mary Theresa was telling us about today's itinerary, her face lit up as she talked about Thika. It was important to her that we liked Thika and felt comfortable and at home in her place of birth.

Thika is an agricultural town, located along the Nyeri Road, about twenty-five miles northwest of Nairobi. This road has the reputation of being the worst in the Nairobi area. All the roads are bad, so ranking this one the worst would be like rating fruitcakes at Christmastime. They're all bad.

Nyeri Road is quite scenic, lined with *shambas* or small farms. Many of the Kenyan tea companies grow their plants along this road.

There is a danger to this ride. This heavily traveled two-lane road is filled with the crazy matatu drivers. Many people commute to work from Thika to Nairobi, and it is not uncommon to see one matatu passing another matatu and nearly causing a head-on collision. Add to that, the Maasai tribesmen with their cows and goats weaving back and forth across the road, and you have yourself quite a ride. Tom had to swerve, once to the right and once to the left, into oncoming traffic, dodging a matatu the first time and a goat the second.

Killing a Maasi's goat is a serious offense. Their goats and cows are their livelihood. The larger their herds, the higher social status they enjoy with their fellow tribesmen. It's not uncommon for the owner of a dead goat to ask the man who killed it for his daughter in payment.

The quickly moving Chania River flows through Thika and eventually gives way to a beautiful waterfall. But if you did not know it was there, you would miss it because the waterfall begins directly under a bridge.

Tom pulled the car into the Blue Post Hotel. The hotel's palm trees, thatched roofs, and aged panel exterior walls made me feel like I was in Hawaii. The 85 percent humidity did not hurt the illusion either.

It was a tourist hotel that had a great view of the Chania River and the falls. Tom showed us to a trail that led down to the falls, which was well-worn but easily navigated. Father Pat decided to stay at the outdoor bar to have a Tusker and a smoke.

The water from the falls became a muddy brown soup as it followed the path of the river.

Any idea of dipping my toes into the water vanished when Tom pointed to a sign that read, "It is prohibited by law to dump cremated remains into the river." Tom just shrugged, and we both had a good laugh, although I thought that it would be a great place to spread my ashes someday.

The beauty of the countryside was in dramatic contrast to the poverty and sickness Father Pat and I had seen thus far. This little side trip was a great break. Tom was taking good care of us.

Back in the car and out to the main road, we traveled west until we came to an unmarked dirt road. The road was crowded with chickens running all over the place and was bordered by open green fields. There was a rusted old frame of an unrecognizable car resting peacefully among the delicate yellow wildflowers.

After beating our kidneys to death dodging chickens and potholes, we arrived at St. Mary Magdalene Church. This is where Sister Mary Theresa manages one of her beloved projects: peer counseling. Teenage leaders are identified by the Catholic schools and by the parish priests and then are trained to teach and counsel their fellow teenagers and preteens on how to avoid becoming infected with and transmitting HIV.

Sister Mary Theresa led us through an open-air church. The altar was built from local timber. The pews were constructed of concrete and placed somewhat at random between tall leafy green trees.

All the church buildings in Kenya must have been painted with the same dirty paint. This church hall was no exception. An old chalkboard hung from the front wall. It was covered with butcher paper outlining the day's subject.

Michael, one of the local youth leaders, had already started his presentation before we walked into the hall. He was a dynamic sixteen-year-old and was the counselor that day. He was wearing a yellow T-shirt, with Archdiocese of Nairobi Peer Counseling silk-screened on the back, and a pair of blue jeans. His tall frame and big eyes demanded attention. This was a good-looking kid who had a very important message to share.

Michael teaching about how to prevent HIV infection.

The room was filled with kids ages ten to eighteen. They were sitting on benches that were positioned in a semicircle around Michael. The kids were wearing the same T-shirt as Michael's.

Michael was pointing to one of the handwritten butcher paper charts on the wall entitled "How to Prevent HIV/AIDS." Under the title were listed the following topics: HIV Modes of Transmission, Implications of HIV/AIDS, Stigmatization, Abstinence and Chastity, and Voluntary Counseling and Testing

Michael spoke English well, and the kids appeared as if they were paying close attention. He had a knack for speaking in front of a large group of kids. Michael's message was clear: Have sex and you will transmit HIV. If you get HIV, it will develop into AIDS, and you will die. His presentation was no nonsense and delivered with the seriousness it deserved.

Michael told the kids that it was everyone's personal responsibility to be tested for HIV. If one believed that they had been exposed, they needed to be tested.

Those who have been infected should be treated with compassion and be helped as much as possible. What Michael, Sister Mary Theresa, and her program were trying to do was to change the culture of death and despair. This would be a tough job.

Abstinence may not be realistic in the Western countries, but it is stressed heavily to the youth in Kenya. It could be the difference between life and death for them.

Condoms are readily available at most gas stations and convenience stores. They are usually sold by the cash register, next to the chewing gum and cigarettes, and are available to all ages. Usually, they come in packs of two with pictures of sexy white women on the package. I purchased a pack and put them in Father Pat's suitcase. He got a good laugh when he found them a couple of days later. In the small towns and villages, there are no convenience stores; abstinence is the only answer to prevent the transmission of HIV.

Outside of the classroom was the youth's fund-raising project. It was raising chicks. No, not girls, but baby chickens. The neighboring farmers bring their newborn chicks and enough food for forty-five days to the parish and under the care of the youth; they raise the chicks to market size. The farmers then sell the chickens and split their profits with the parish.

The chicken pen was the most modern structure I had seen so far: cinder block foundation, four-by-four beams, and braces. There were new food and water dispensers for the chicks' hygienic environment. One had to step into a shallow pool of disinfectant before walking into the pen. Father Pat found humor in the fact that the chicks are kept in a cleaner environment than the kids.

This project helped fund the peer counseling program as well as helping provide monies needed to the parents of over three hundred retarded children the parish looks after. Yes, three hundred retarded children in a very small community. The parish priest, Father Samuel, was at a loss to explain the high incidence of retardation with the children. The government, although aware of it, has neither the resources nor the interest in investigating the issue.

*   *   *

The next day was Sunday, and Sister Mary Theresa intended for us to spend the night in Thika and for Father Pat to preside over the Mass. The problem was that neither I nor Father Pat knew that we were staying overnight in Thika until Sister Mary Theresa mentioned it in passing as we left the church. Plus, neither one of us had packed for a stay overnight.

Politely, Father Pat said that we were not staying. That he had not packed for an overnight stay because he did not know about it.

I don't know what Sister Mary Theresa said to him, but it made him angry. Father Pat said in a voice loud enough for all around to hear him, "I am sleeping in the same bed tonight that I slept in last night." That was the end of the conversation.

In retrospect, Father Pat said that Sister Mary Theresa may have mentioned it to him on our arrival at the Norfolk Hotel, but he did not remember it. I then felt bad because it was my job to keep those things straight. I also had the feeling that Sister Mary Theresa had a reception and dinner planned in our honor that night. Father Pat, at sixty-three years old, paced himself very well. Besides, he and I are both party-poopers; so if there was one, we were not sorry to have missed it.

Heading back to Nairobi, Edward, our cameraman, wanted to stop in downtown Thika to take some film for the documentary he was putting together. Downtown Thika was filled with two-story, unreinforced masonry buildings that were in dire need of painting. Everything in Nairobi and Thika was in dire need of a paint job.

As we saw in most towns and cities we visited, the downtown area gave you the impression of a vibrant, hustling city. There were people everywhere, walking every which way. The natives had grocery bags in hand; there were women carrying woven baskets on the top of their heads. But I still had a question: where the hell was everyone going?

It was difficult to drive because of all the people, but Tom found a parking spot; and Edward went out to shoot his film. I decided to go with him.

Edward set up his tripod and camera on the corner of a busy street. We were next to a newsstand that carried most of the magazines that one would find in the United States: *Time, Newsweek*, and the supermarket rags, *National Enquirer* and *Weekly World News*. Most of them were several months old. There were also dozens of African newspapers and magazines.

I was looking around, taking in all the sights. Across the street was a park with dead grass and a once-white gazebo. Old men were sitting inside it, taking a break from smoking cigarettes and the warm sun. At least a hundred kids were running around the park, with no parents to be found; some were playing soccer with a nearly flat soccer ball; some were playing tag.

I was standing at the intersection of a four-way stop. From my vantage point, I could see down all four converging streets. Each street looked the same: they were crowded with hundreds of black people, their heads bobbing up and down with the rhythm of their stride, all lined with faded buildings, some with bars over the windows.

In my mind, I was trying to picture what this city looked like in its heyday—when the kids were clean and clothed properly and most of the adults had a job and did not have to worry about how they were going to feed their family that day. I then thought that maybe Thika never had a heyday. I was pulled back to reality by a tug on the back of my shirt.

I turned around, and there, standing in front of me, was a little boy about six years old. His face was so thin, and his eyes were sunken right into the back of his head. His hair was very short and dirty. I was sure I saw lice jumping from it. He looked and smelled as though he had not washed in weeks. He was wearing old cotton sweatpants and a dusty tan winter jacket even though it was at least ninety degrees where we were standing. He was thrusting his muddy hands, with skin peeling from his fingers, into my chest and begging for money.

Edward pulled the child aside and had a conversation with him. I was watching them intently, not knowing what they were saying to each other because they were speaking Swahili. Edward was talking to the boy so easily that one might think that he was friends with him. His gentle manner made me think that Edward would be a great father someday.

The boy turned from Edward and walked back to me. He reached deep into his right pocket and brought out all the coins he had. He tried to give me all his money. He was also trying to tell me something. His dusty face was smiling, but his gestures and words were beyond me.

"What is he saying, Edward?" I inquired. "What did you say to him?"

"I told him that you were a visitor to our country and that it was impolite for him to ask you for money," Edward explained. "Since you are a visitor, he is trying to give you all of his money so you can get something to eat."

My heart swelled, and my eyes began to tear up. I hugged the boy and asked Edward to tell him thank you but for him to keep his money. I then reached into my pocket and pulled about one thousand four hundred shillings, about twenty U.S. dollars, and gave it to the boy.

"Asante! Asante sana!" the little boy kept saying over and over. He then said that he would pray for me. Imagine that, he was going to pray for me.

This was the kind of hospitality that I saw and experienced the entire two weeks in Kenya. They were warm and friendly people concerned more with taking care of their guests than taking care of their own needs.

Chapter 6

Njoroge and Kamau

Our first Sunday in Kenya started out as an amazing day; we were awakened by several Marabou storks. The Marabou stork is common in Nairobi, like pigeons are common in most cities in the United States. This bird looks like a cross between a toucan and a pelican. Their large banana-shaped beaks and long necks made the Marabou look like it could never get its awkward black, white, and yellow body off the ground. They have an annoying cry that sounds more like a cow in heat. Okay, I have never heard a cow in heat, but I would imagine that is what it would sound like. The Marabou stork was our alarm clock most mornings.

There was a peacefulness that morning at the convent that was hard to describe. The high wall surrounding the convent effectively cloisters the grounds from the outside world. Sitting on a bench, under a huge yellow-and-green leafy tree, left me with a feeling of contentment.

I allowed my mind to wander, and I began to think of all the illness and suffering we had seen so far. But amid all of that, I witnessed loving support and a deep caring for one another. That would be one of the little tidbits that I would take away with me from this trip.

As usual, Tom was right on time, and we were quickly on our way to Kiambu. Tom dazzled us with his encyclopedic knowledge of the Kikuyu tribe. In one of the rare moments that he and I did not talk politics, he told me a little about the Kikuyu people.

The Kikuyu people migrated to the Nairobi area nearly four centuries ago. They were, and still are, successful farmers raising various types of crops. The Kikuyu were the main participants in the Mau Mau Rebellion in the 1950s, laying the foundation for Kenya's independence. As I mentioned before, Jomo Kenyatta, Kenya's first president, was a Kikuyu.

There have been many changes in the lives of all the tribes of Kenya since their independence, but one characteristic remains the same. The strength of the Kikuyu is still the family.

Before independence, groups of families would come together on the farms and work for the benefit of the whole group. Even today, family unity remains at the center of their daily lives.

In the past, if a male wanted to leave the family unit, he could become a warrior, with responsibility of protecting the tribe. The rite of passage of becoming a warrior included circumcision.

Women had a similar right of passage: female circumcision.[9] In the past, this public ritual signified one's passage to womanhood. It was a tribal custom to signify that a girl was ready to be married. It was believed that if the woman was circumcised, it would remove her sexual desire, and she would then always be faithful to her husband.

Still today, 30 percent of Kikuyu women are circumcised. There is a tremendous amount of pressure from the government and outside groups to stop this barbaric mutilation. Progress is being made, but it is very slow. The United Nations classifies this ritual as female genital mutilation.

*   *   *

For some weeks, prior to our trip, Father Pat had talked about experiencing a real African Catholic Mass. After yesterday's disagreement with Sister Mary Theresa, we were not sure where we would go to Mass, but she came through for us. Making some quick arrangements by cell phone, she talked to Father Simon of St. Peter and Paul Catholic Church in Kiambu.

Kiambu is a town located ten miles northeast of Nairobi. Kiambu is a bedroom community with a population of about five thousand people, mostly from the Kikuyu tribe.

The main street was paved, but there were no sidewalks; and the streets were lined with mango and papaya trees. Many of the side streets off the main drag were winding dirt roads with potholes large enough to lose a small car in. This was my kind of town.

We arrived at 9:30 a.m. and parked on the street. There were already a lot of cars parked all around the church.

---

[9]   Female circumcision is a procedure where a respected woman from the tribe will remove the clitoris from a woman who is ready to marry.

Sister Mary Theresa took us to meet Father Simon. He was a dead ringer for Apollo Creed, played by Carl Weathers in several of the *Rocky* movies. He was even built like a boxer, about six feet two and two hundred pounds—solid as a rock.

Father Simon quickly fitted Father Pat with an alb[10] and asked him to celebrate the Mass. I was not happy when Father Simon asked me to give a five-minute speech at the end of Mass. I have never met a microphone I didn't like, but I was not prepared to speak in a church full of Kikuyus. I was thinking, *Hell, I would now have to spend most of the Mass trying to come up with something intelligent to say.*

Father Simon led us around the back of the church to join the entrance procession. There must have been seventy-five people in the line. Needless to say, it was the longest procession I have ever seen.

I joked with Sister Christine that the entire congregation must be standing in the line.

She said, "Just wait until we get inside the church; you may be surprised."

Yeah, sure, I thought.

When the music started, the people in the procession started singing and dancing. I felt so out of place. I have no rhythm, and I can't sing. I am very white. But what I quickly found out is that they didn't care. So I clapped and bobbed and weaved along with the natives, looking just like a white guy trying to be black. I felt like Steve Martin in *Bringing Down the House*, when he went to rescue Queen Latifah. That was me.

I nearly fell over when I walked inside the church. There were eight hundred to nine hundred people in that building, all clapping hands, singing, and dancing. The music was so rhythmic and professional sounding I was sure it was recorded, but it was coming from a live band. It had a seven-piece drum kit, bongo drums, and a piano. I had never heard anything like it before. It was fantastic.

Any experience in Africa and especially Kenya is not complete without experiencing the vibrant colors and the rhythms of its people; this Mass was that experience.

There were eight-hundred-plus people dressed in their very best. As I tried to dance down the main aisle, everyone was staring at me but not with that "What the hell is he doing here?" stare. Their eyes, smiles, and hands were all welcoming. Taking my seat on the side of the alter, I had a good look at the people who were ready to celebrate Mass.

To these people, Mass is not a Sunday obligation; it is a welcomed celebration. The women sitting next to me were wearing *bu bu's* (like Hawaiian *muu muus*) made of beautiful *kentenge* (cotton), displaying every vivid color of the rainbow and every pattern one could imagine. They also wore matching kentenge headbands. The men wore more traditional Western business suits and were a bit more reserved in their celebration.

---

10   Robe that Catholic priests wear during Mass.

The enthusiasm of the women was breathtaking. Their bodies almost seemed to form exquisite musical notes as they moved to the rhythms flowing from the instruments of the spirited and creative musicians.

This, of course, made me even more self-conscious. I can't explain why I could not loosen up. I guess that my senses were overwhelmed. Here, for the first time in my life, I was experiencing what I had always envisioned what church could be like: a strong sense of community and a Sunday worship that was more of a celebration of life than a weekly obligation.

These people have so little, but at the same time, they have an inner peace—a relationship with their God, which is special and unique.

The great thing about the Catholic Mass is that the ritual, the readings, and the prayers are all the same around the world. It is what each culture brings to the Mass that makes it unique.

The presentation of the gospel was breathtaking. Fourteen girls, ages eight to twelve, came dancing down the center aisle, with the tallest girl at the back of the procession carrying the Book of Gospels above her head. The congregation was on their feet. The girls were dancing to the beat of the drums in their pink T-shirts and multicolored wraps with their heads, shoulders, and feet moving in unison. The house was rockin'!

Just before the end of the Mass, it was my turn to get up and talk to the people. I walked up to the podium, looked out at the people, and my eyes started to tear up.

This is just great, I said to myself. *There are eight hundred people out there, and I'm going to break down.*

I was able to gather myself, and I began to speak, "Thank you very much for welcoming us to your country and your church. Everywhere Father Pat and I have traveled, we have felt so welcomed. Today I would like to speak to you about the youth in your country. The future of your country is in good hands. Your youth are strong and smart."

Then I told them about the little boy in Thika. Everyone in the church made that "oh" sound, you know, the one people make when one sees a cute newborn baby.

I thought that my speech was a little corny, but it did the job; and the best part was that it made Father Simon very happy.

After I took my seat, Father Simon rose and asked the congregation if they thought that Father Pat and I should be initiated into the Kikuyu tribe. The congregation gave out a huge cheer. Separately, both Father Pat and I had hoped for something like this because we felt it would signify that we had made a positive connection with the people of Kenya. We were overjoyed, and so were the people in the church.

"So," started Father Simon, "since Father Pat is older, we will make him a Kikuyu elder. What name shall we give him?" he asked.

"Kamau," someone from the back of the church yelled. "Kamau, it is," Father Simon said. "In the Kikuyu language, *Kamau* means the Resurrected One."

"Since Mike is young, we will make him a warrior." Young, I guess, is relative since I was forty-three years old. I started laughing, and I'm sure that a few of the people in church were laughing too.

Before Father Simon could even ask, a retarded man sitting in a chair in front of the first pew yelled out, "Njoroge." Everyone laughed. Father Simon said that *Njoroge* means "the Lovely One." Father Pat laughed so hard that he nearly passed out. Father Simon invited everyone to meet at the front of the church for the ceremony.

The church was built in the traditional Catholic style. It was shaped like a cross, with the entryway at the foot of the cross with several stairs leading up to the door.

While we waited for the ceremony to begin, Father Pat invited the children to be blessed and to bless him. I was quite content today to just stand to the side and watch the smiles and the wonderment on the faces of these beautiful children. The girls wore brightly colored dresses and arranged their hair in cornrows. The boys wore their Sunday best, some wearing ties. Their hair was cropped very close to their heads.

Father Pat blesses a little girl at Kiambu.

One little girl, about six years old, with long cornrows, came up to Father Pat. Her big round eyes were fixed on his face. She sure was curious. I could tell she wanted to touch his face but was just too shy. Father Pat blessed her, and that gave her the opening to touch his face. She blessed him and then laid her palm against his cheek.

Because priests are held in such high regard in Kenya and it was unusual to receive a blessing like the way Father Pat does it, I was sure that this was an important moment in her young life.

Father Pat was in his element. He loves kids, and kids love him back. He could have sat on those steps and blessed the children all day.

An elderly gentleman, I would guess about seventy years old, dressed in an old blue suit was in charge of the ceremony. He must have been a Kikuyu elder and, I'm willing to bet, took part in the Mau Mau Rebellion as a warrior back in the mid-1950s.

He brought with him a three-legged stool, which was painted black and decorated with yellow flowers; a three-foot stick; and a four-inch gourd connected to a chain. The elder explained that the three-legged stool was a sign of respect. At one time, when the council of elders would meet, each elder would sit on one of these little stools.

He put the stool down and asked Father Pat to sit. Then he presented him with a talking stick. This is a three-foot stick that is rounded at the top. It is passed around the circle of elders, and the one holding the stick was allowed to speak. The next gift given to Father Pat was a cow's tail. Father Pat and I both thought that this was an item of great importance. As the elder explained, it *was* important. It was used to swat the flies away.

Father Pat, Kikuyu Elder

Finally, there was the gourd, which is worn around the neck of an elder so he always has his snuff with him. Father Pat was now officially an elder of the Kikuyu tribe.

Then I was called to the top of the stairs. The elder said that the first and most important ritual of becoming a warrior was circumcision. Everyone laughed.

"Yeah right," I said. "That was taken care of forty-two years ago."

Everyone laughed again. The elder apologized that he did not have the real tools of a warrior because this was all on such short notice. But he presented me with a spear, made from a tree branch; a shield, which was the top of a woven basket; a rusty old knife; a cow-tail flyswatter; and a walking stick.

Then another old man about four and a half feet tall came over, took my tree branch, and demonstrated how to use it. He turned a little sideways, bent a little at the knees, with his right leg slightly in front of his left. He took the spear back behind his ear and made a

The Kikuyu warrior.

throwing motion with his arm. He was very excited and was speaking so fast I could not understand him. It also didn't help that he was speaking Kikuyu or Swahili.

We were given quite an ovation. I estimated that a couple of hundred people stayed around to watch. Pictures were taken with the elders; and then Father Simon invited us to his house for lunch, which consisted of rice, beans, peas, carrots, and chicken served in those same plastic containers we saw at Judy's house.

At lunch, we met Father Simon's assistant Deacon Edward. He was a transitional deacon, which is the last step before being ordained as a priest. Edward was an interesting man, with a large head, slightly out of proportion with the rest of his body. Edward was very well educated, and he told us that he was looking forward to his ordination the following May.

After lunch, Father Simon took us to see the new school he just built for the local children. It was a U-shaped two-story building with a beautiful garden in the back. The children had planted several varieties of fruits and vegetables. These were used to provide breakfast and lunch for the children. The children were also taught how to tend to the garden. This is a skill that would immediately come in handy with their families.

Father Simon invited us back to his church someday, where he promised to have all of the possessions ready for me, the new Kikuyu warrior.

This was a very special day. Father Pat proclaimed, while we were driving back to the convent, that this was an experience he so much wanted to have. I agreed with him. To feel the beat and rhythm of the Kikuyu and to make the connection we made were tremendously satisfying.

Chapter 7

The Road to Machakos

Leaving Nairobi for an overnight trip to Machakos, I purchased a copy of the *Daily Nation*. Its front-page story told a bone-chilling story of how dangerous Nairobi can be.

A woman was abducted on a matatu by being rendered unconscious from an injection of some substance that was administered by a man standing next to her. The woman was taken to an unknown place.

When she woke up, she found herself in a room with three other sedated but conscious women. The four women were shown a closet that contained the hanging skinned bodies of other women. These four captive women were told to take their clothes off and that they would be raped. If they refused, they would end up like the women hanging in the closet. Upon seeing these skinned human beings, one woman vomited and another passed out. The third woman refused to take her clothes off even after her captor—a woman, believe it or not—held a gun to her head. She still refused and was immediately shot dead through the head. The other women in the room were made to drink a bowl of blood from the murdered woman. The three then capitulated and had sex with their captors.

Two days later, the women were released to the streets of Nairobi. One woman came forward to the newspapers because when she went to the police station, the police officer told her that he would not help her unless she had sex with him.

After reading this story, I was in shock. I relayed the info to Tom, and he said that there were still many black-magic cults in Kenya and this was one of their rituals. The police, he said, had been holding back helping women for years unless they were willing to have sex with them.

After seeing what I had seen thus far, I believe that these are the kinds of issues that the government of Kenya was going to have to clean up before they could get the total confidence of the people.

*　　*　　*

The city of Machakos is located about twenty miles southeast of Nairobi. The road we took, Highway A109, is actually known as the road to Mombassa. It was newly paved about one hundred years ago.

You can be assured that the bad roads did not discourage the matatu drivers. These guys should be driving in NASCAR events. The drivers demonstrated great skill; knowledge of the location of every pothole; and the reckless abandon of a person without fear for themselves, their passengers, or the drivers heading in the opposite direction.

The matatus were not only stuffed with people, but there were also people hanging off the rear bumpers and out of the sliding side door. They also had luggage stacked seven or eight feet high. I was tempted to ask one of the drivers how he was able to tie the luggage down so well, but I never got close enough.

One matatu went flying by us with a man sitting on top of four suitcases tied to the luggage rack on top. A second one passed us with a wild-eyed live goat riding on top, having, I'm sure, the ride of its life.

It had not rained here in a long time; dust was flying everywhere. Tall black men and weathered-looking women—with short cropped hair, wearing faded dresses—were walking along the side of the road with large baskets balanced on their heads, containing fruit, rice, and clothing.

Have you ever seen dusty, dry palm trees? I never had before, but there they were. As I contemplated the ragged-looking palm trees, Tom suddenly had to slam on the brakes of the Land Cruiser to avoid hitting a stray cow from a herd being tended by a Maasai shepherd. He was dressed in traditional clothing; a red blanket was wrapped around his waist and over his right shoulder that amazingly covered all the necessary parts.

His woman was with him, wearing a matching blanket with her breasts bouncing along in all their glory. It was my dancing black breasts—a *National Geographic* moment!

Huge colorful rings made their earlobes hang just inches from their shoulders. His arms and wrists were covered with gold and silver jewelry as he carried a seven-foot carved walking stick.

The Maasai are one of Kenya's last tribal people. Some dress Western style with dusty slacks and old Goodwill rejected shirts, but most of the Maasai dress in their traditional blankets and jewelry.

The Massai don't eat their cows. The animals are part of their families. These native tribesmen live on the blood and milk from their cows.

So, dear, how about a cocktail?

That sounds wonderful, honey. Would you like your milk mixed with the blood or on the side?

Yuck!

Tom told us that it was not that long ago that you would see giraffes grazing on the tall trees along the road. Now there were no giraffes and no trees either. The giraffes were gone because the locals had cut all the trees down to use as firewood and to build houses.

The oddest thing we saw along the road to Machakos, and maybe the oddest thing I had ever seen, was the style of coffins being manufactured at a roadside coffin company. Not ones of beautifully carved oak with shiny brass trim. These were boxes made from metal. The boxes were shaped like a traditional coffin but with a slot on the top that was positioned just right so that the person in the coffin could "see out." The hole is there to double-check to make sure the dude in the box is actually dead.

Rolling into Machakos was like rolling into an old Western outpost. The streets had wooden sidewalks, and many of the buildings looked like they were built from adobe and wood. I was expecting to see John Wayne walk out into the street.

Machakos is Akamba territory. The woodcarvings from Kenya are mostly crafted by the Akamba tribe. They were also known to the British as tremendous fighters and were put on the front lines in Europe by the British during World War I. Needless to say, thousands of the Akamba people lost their lives during the war. Today, they are a peaceful people and live mostly in and south of the Machakos Valley area.

Machakos is Agnes's hometown. You remember Agnes from chapter 2, with the Goodyear blimp-sized breasts? She was waiting for us at the cathedral. It was not weird that Agnes was there because she lived close by in the hills above the city, but it *was* weird that she appeared in every place we went. Agnes did not drive and did not know what our schedule was, but she was always there. At the cathedral in Nairobi, at Korogocho, and at the convent, Agnes was always there.

Agnes had told us, earlier in our trip, that she was excited that we would be visiting the cathedral in Machakos. It is her home parish, and she wanted us to see where she worshiped and volunteered her time with the parish children.

Sister Mary Theresa arranged for Father Charles, the bishop's secretary, and Francis Mwunga, the diocese development director, to meet us.

Francis's secretary showed us to his large office. She was a sweet petite woman, with a smile as big as Machakos itself. She told us that she lived on the outskirts of Machakos, with a view of the Machakos Valley. She showed us to a couple of well-worn leather chairs in Francis's office and quickly excused herself.

As I was telling Father Pat how tired I was and how I was hoping for an early night and a good sleep, Francis and Father Charles came in carrying bottles of Coca-Cola for each of us.

Damn, it was warm Coke. It was nearly undrinkable, but since my mouth felt like it had been sucking on a dusty rock for the last two hours, I drank it anyway.

Francis began to tell us about the various problems he was facing as the development director.

"Money is always a problem. Machakos is a thriving city in comparison to most cities in Kenya, but the poverty continues. Although our AIDS infection rate is not as high as Nairobi, it is still creating orphans faster than we can keep up with them."

"Francis," I started, "when HIV and AIDS became known in the United States, it was first thought to be a homosexual disease until more research was done and we found out that everyone was at risk. How much of the infection rate in Kenya can be attributed to homosexuality?" His answer nearly knocked me on my ass.

After glancing at Father Charles, Francis said, "There are no homosexuals in Kenya."

Father Pat and I looked at each other in disbelief. "There are no homosexuals in Kenya?" Father Pat repeated.

"That's correct, Pat," Father Charles said in a tone of voice that sounded like he was trying to convince himself. He repeated, hoping that would end the conversation, "There are no homosexuals in Kenya."

There was no way that Father Pat or I were going to let these two guys off the hook.

Father Pat continued, "The homosexual population in the world is about 1 percent, and you're telling us that there are no gays here?"

Francis dug his hole a little deeper, "It is not allowed."

"Ah, come on," I jumped in, "what are you talking about? It's not allowed?" I was becoming quite agitated because I felt that denying that gays existed was not only ignorant and discriminatory, but it was going to hamper efforts to get a handle on the AIDS problem.

The two of them stood their ground, and I could see that Father Pat was becoming quite excited because he was beginning to gesticulate wildly. "You guys are in denial. There is no way that the population of homosexuals is different in Kenya than it is in the rest of the world."

With us, this now became more of an issue of gays in Kenya instead of the AIDS infection rate.

Father Charles finally broke the standoff, "Homosexuality is not open here in Kenya like it is in the States. There may be homosexuals here, but we don't know how many."

"Father Charles, what's the real issue here?" I pressed.

Francis jumped in, "If you are caught in a homosexual act, you will be stoned or beaten to death; so as you can see, homosexual behavior is not allowed here."

This country, or at least these two guys, was going to have to come to grips with the fact that homosexuality is a fact of life. If this was the prevailing attitude of the people in Kenya, then a huge cultural change was needed before the AIDS epidemic can be controlled.

"You have to realize Kenya is not like the United States," Francis added.

Father Pat and I both smiled. Father Pat told me later that when Francis said that, he nearly blurted out, "THANK GOD!"

This was not the way we wanted our visit in Machakos to start, but we had made our point that we were not going to take the information we were given at face value.

Father Charles said it was time for us to head to the pastoral center, where we could drop off our bags, freshen up, and then meet Bishop Martin for lunch.

Our room was in a building that was designed for men studying for the priesthood. The pastoral center was also part of the seminary. The building was empty. Father Pat and I would share one room, and Tom would have a room to himself.

I had to chuckle when we walked into our room. The beds were covered with mosquito netting. I could have used this at home. I always had a pesky little mosquito in my bedroom, which would fly around my ear, sounding like a B-52 bomber right before it landed on my skin to suck my blood.

The netting looked like fun and made for a great picture. It made it look like we were actually roughing it.

Keeping the mosquitoes out.

After washing up, we headed to Bishop Martin's house. He was a very popular priest in the Machakos district and had been ordained as bishop only six months before. At forty-five years old, he was a little young to be a bishop. Father Charles said that Bishop Martin had a commanding presence, and he seemed to be enjoying all the attention he was receiving as the new bishop of Machakos.

When we walked into his house and dining room, Father Pat and I started to laugh because there, on the table, were the same five Tupperware-like containers that we saw at Judy's house on our first day in Nairobi. And would you believe it, they were filled with almost the same things: chicken, beans, rice, thick soup, and a thick gravylike substance with peas and carrots mixed in.

That afternoon, we headed to a school called the Better Center, run by the development office. It is there where we met the most boring man in the universe: Mr. Mbugnu. In his younger days, he must have taught personality classes to rocks. The bad thing about this was that he was in charge of the Better Center. Mr. Mbugnu was about five feet five and 140 pounds. He wore a pair of Fingerhut-style double-knit brown slacks and a brown-and-yellow plaid jacket. He looked like he just stepped off the bus from 1975.

The Better Center is a secondary boarding school, grades 9-12, where the kids learn the three *R*s and a skill. The girls learn how to sew and do leatherwork. The boys learn how to be auto mechanics.

When we arrived at the center, we were greeted by Agnes's daughter, Florence.

Florence was thirty-three years old but looked like she was about twelve. She was very tiny, maybe four feet two and eighty-five pounds. She taught English and lived on the school property. She had a nice cinder block house that was about fifty-by-twenty feet. It was a palace compared to most of the homes we saw in Machakos.

We met with Mr. Mbugnu and his teaching staff. When we walked into the conference room, eight teachers and Mr. Mbugnu were sitting around a table. Florence introduced us to everyone.

I thought we had just walked into the middle of a funeral. There were so many sad faces that I wanted to ask who the hell died.

Most of the people we had met, at least up to this point, were happy to talk to us and tell us about their problems and challenges. Mr. Mbugnu did tell us about his school's problems, but he nearly put us to sleep doing it. No one else said a word. They just sat there watching the bubbles rise in their hot Coca-Cola.

Have you ever heard the old maxim that a team can take on the personality of its coach? That was what happened at the Better Center.

Father Pat started asking questions, and all he received back from the teachers were blank stares. I think the teachers did not want to speak up with Mr. Mbugnu in the room. When he got up to get more hot soda, one of the teachers told us that the school was in dire need of money. The tuition for a year is four hundred dollars; and that covers room, board, and school fees. The teachers received a percentage of the tuition, and because enrollment was down, many teachers were having problems making a living.

There were many students that were having trouble coming up with the tuition, but the school was doing its best to keep those kids enrolled.

Mr. Mbugnu came back with warm cola and warm Orange Fanta. Most places we visited, we were offered warm soda. This place could barely afford the essentials, and giving us warm soda, or any soda for that matter, was silly. But this is how the Kenyans are; even people with the personality of a crescent wrench wanted to make sure that their guests are taken care of.

"Have you contacted some of the bigger companies in the area to see if they would be interested in giving scholarships or sponsoring a student?" I asked.

"No" was the answer.

"Have you asked any companies if they are interested in hiring interns so when the kids get out of school, they already have work experience and have an inside track for a job?"

We got another big fat no from Mr. Mbugnu. The teachers seemed to be warming up because we were starting to drill their boss pretty hard.

"Mr. Mbugnu," Father Pat continued, "the answer to your money problems seem to be out there. You need to get out from behind your desk and start knocking on doors."

With that, Mbugnu jumped up, moving faster than we had yet seen him, and asked us if we would like a tour.

It was difficult not to make fun of Mr. Mbugnu because he sounded like he was in pain every time he talked. Both Father Pat and I wanted to get this over quickly because Mr. Personality was driving us nuts. The tour began in the showers and the latrine. Mind you, Machakos has been in the middle of a drought for quite some time. The latrines consisted of cinder block stalls with a hole in the middle of the floor with a brick on each side to put your feet on. I'm telling you, if the flies did not get you, the smell did.

At the end of the tour, Mr. Mbugnu asked if we had any questions, and Father Pat asked if we could see the latrines again. The sarcasm was lost on Mr. Mbugnu.

We thanked Mr. Mbugnu for his hospitality, jumped into the Land Cruiser, and told Tom to drive us away as fast as he could.

Upon arriving back at the pastoral center, we were met by Father Charles again. I was relieved that we had not offended him with our earlier conversation about homosexuals. I was also glad to see him because we weren't sure what was going on with dinner.

Father Pat and I would have been happy to order room service and watch some TV. Yeah right, maybe if we were staying at the Kenya Hilton but not at the pastoral center in the outskirts of Machakos.

"Francis wants to take you three out to dinner tonight. He will pick you up at six. Just meet him out front," Father Charles said as he made sure that we were settled in our rooms and then left us for the evening.

"There's a restaurant around here?" I asked to no one in particular. I hadn't seen any place where I would want to eat. This was going to be interesting.

Francis came by in his beat-up Toyota Corolla, and we piled in for the fifteen-minute ride to downtown Machakos. Most of the workers had made their way home already, and the city was fairly quiet. It was evident that Machakos did not have the street-children problem that Nairobi did or have the thriving nightlife that Nairobi did either.

Francis rambled into the parking lot of the Ikuuni Hotel, located in the middle of a little strip mall. There were six guys milling around outside a bar. If we were in the United States, I would have thought that they were looking for trouble, but the men were all very absorbed in their own conversation. We walked by these dirty, smelly men without incident.

I was rather surprised at how nice the restaurant was. I would have preferred more interior light, but the romantic atmosphere would have to do. We were the only ones in the place.

Our waiter and bus woman were very friendly and tended to everything, always wearing a bright huge smile. I'm sure they were just happy that someone came into the restaurant. Francis told us that this restaurant attracted the "better-off people" on the weekends, but it was somewhat quiet during the week. He also said that during the summer, the rooms above the restaurant were a popular place for Europeans and Americans to stay.

Francis also surprised us by saying that he lived at the cathedral during the week and on the weekend traveled three hours one way—to the jungle where his wife and eight kids lived. They had no running water or electricity. He hoped that he could move his family to the city someday, but he enjoyed the simple weekends; and he also loved his neighbors.

"We are all Akamba out in the village. It is a simple and satisfying life. But I need a job, and this was the closest one I could find. It helps keep my kids in shoes and food on the table."

"Eight kids!" Father Pat said. "Did anyone ever tell you what caused that?" Once again, Father Pat's sarcasm was lost on Francis. But Tom thought it was funny, and he nearly spit out the mouthful of Tusker he was drinking.

Our waiter came by to take our order. I'm usually adventurous when it comes to food, but the faces of all those people back home who warned me that I would get sick in Kenya kept popping into my head. "I'll have the baked chicken." I had seen chickens running around the streets of Machakos, so they must be fresh.

"He'll have the goat ribs," Father Pat butted in.

So I had the goat ribs.

I'm glad that he ordered them for me because they were sweet and delicious. And just in case you were wondering, they did not taste like chicken. We also ordered a side dish of peas. What we did not know was that the side dish was about four pounds of peas. They were mixed with something. I don't know what it was; but again, they were rich, tender, and covered with a spicy, sticky sauce.

After dinner and three Tuskers, we were ready for bed.

Francis enjoyed our company. I don't think he does much after work. So taking us out to dinner was a treat for him.

There must not be drunken-driving laws in Kenya because Francis had quite a few beers himself and was in no shape to drive, but somehow, he got us to the pastoral center safely.

It felt good to be back in our room. The courtyard by our building was alive with people laughing and talking. The seminarians that lived in the building across from us had just finished a prayer service and were heading back to their rooms.

The mosquito netting proved to be quite a challenge. I kept rolling into the net, and there was a mosquito buzzing around the room most of the night, keeping me awake anyway. Father Pat was sure that that mosquito was inside his net. I was never so happy to see the sunrise and glad to see that I was still alive. I was sure that the goat I ate the night before was going to kill me.

After untangling myself from the netting, I quickly dressed because I wanted to head outside and see the sunrise in the valley. To my horror, the door to the building was locked from the outside. How stupid was that? If there was an emergency, we would not have been able to get out, except by throwing a chair through the window.

After knocking on the door for a few minutes, a guard unlocked and opened the door. Although he was wearing a khaki uniform and looked like a security guard, he scared the shit out of me with the eight-inch rusty knife he was holding.

So we were locked in a building all night being guarded by a man with every other tooth missing and a rusty old knife. Welcome to Kenya!

I took a walk to the other end of the compound just as the sun began to crest above the valley. There were patches of rain clouds at the east end of the Machakos Valley. I plopped down on a rock and watched one of the most beautiful sunrises I had ever seen. The cool air danced on my face. I felt in harmony with the life in the valley and at peace with myself.

After the sun lit most of the valley, I used my binoculars to see if I could find any wildlife. No luck for me today.

Upon returning to my room, Father Pat was in the shower, so I decided to find Tom's room. He was packing his stuff when I got there.

"How long have you been up, Tom?"

"Since about five thirty. I always wake up early."

"Did you see the sunrise?"

"No, I always read scripture early in the morning."

That was Tom. He was a very spiritual, Bible-based man. But he never preached to us and never quoted the Bible. He just lived his life the best way he could.

After getting cleaned up, we all took a walk around the seminary. To the joy of the natives, it started to rain. We jumped into the first building we saw; it turned out to be a chapel, and Mass was just beginning. We stood in the back of the room and missed hearing the readings and the homily by the priest because of the constant beat of the rain on the metal rooftop. We were happy for the people of Machakos because it had not rained for a long, long time.

Heading back to our rooms, we met Sister Josephina. She told us she was eighty-two years old and that she was one of the original Assumption sisters. Father Pat asked her if she knew our friend Bernadette who was an original Assumption sister too.

"Is she black or brown?" asked Sister Josephina.

Father Pat and I both started laughing. "Black or brown, aren't you all brown?"

"No," Sister said. She was a little perplexed at our question. "Some of us are blacker than others."

Sister started telling us about the history of how Bishop J. J. McCarthy started the Assumption sisters. After a few minutes, I kind of tuned her out and was ready to go. Father Pat was having a great conversation with her. It was almost like they had been in the convent together. The religious seem to have some kind of fraternity thing going on. It always seems like old-home week even if they just met.

I left Father Pat and Sister Josephina and headed back to our room. I was ready to hit the road and get the day started.

Chapter 8

Turning Trash into Cash

We had one more stop before we left Machakos, and that was to visit Florence's twin sister, Theresa, at her place of business: Machakos Export, where Theresa was a buyer. The company employed about ten people and, as their name implies, exports goods to Europe and the United States.

Agnes met us at the store, and it was easy to see that she was proud of Theresa. She showed us around their modest building and then took us to their small storefront so I could purchase a few items to take home. The company specialized in wood carvings and woven baskets.

Being in the heart of Akamba territory, it was easy for the company to contract with local artists, some living out in the bush, to hand carve various figures of animals, Maasai men and women, Kikuyu elders, Akamba warriors, walking canes, etc. The pieces are beautiful works of art. If the artists lived in a first-world country, their talents would be much in demand. The carvings in this shop could easily sell for twenty-five to three hundred dollars each in the United States, but in Machakos, they averaged about two dollars each. We filled up a suitcase for about two hundred dollars. This was a big sale for the store. They were extremely happy to see us.

Agnes asked Father Pat if he would carry a few carved wooden lions home to give to her friends back in the States. He agreed but failed to tell me that I was paying for them. When the woman went to total my purchase, Agnes told her to add hers to mine.

"Father Pat told me that you would buy these for me," said Agnes. What could I say?

It was no big deal, and Father Pat got a good laugh from the surprised look on my face.

We loaded up our purchases and left a trail of dust behind us, which added to the dust already covering the town.

Just outside the city of Machakos was the home of Mary, the oldest of Agnes's eleven children. Mary wanted us to have lunch at her home before we left Machakos. Mary was hell-bent, trying to impress Father Pat. As I mentioned earlier, this was a great example of why Father Pat did not usually disclose that he is a Catholic priest; people weirded out on him. And Mary was "weirding" out. She was always talking about her accomplishments and was constantly trying to teach Father Pat about the Holy Scriptures.

Mary also was a "close talker," at least when she was around Father Pat. I did not know if she wanted to kiss him, date him, or wanted him to admire her breath. It was odd watching Father Pat's reaction. In the past, I've seen him cut a person like Mary off at the knees; but out of love and respect for Agnes, he played Mary's game very well.

She was not Catholic, but it was clear that she was a member of some Christian denomination. Mary had a very nice home but did not have running water in the house, and her food was prepared in a dirty kitchen[11] by her hired help. Mary was very well-off. She owned a farm, a store, and a primary school.

One of the nicest things about our visit to Mary's was to see Agnes's niece Esther again. We had met Esther the year before when she visited the United States. She is tall, slender, and gorgeous. Esther wore her hair in cornrows, and she has soft, silky black completion. Her almond-shaped black eyes are so dark that you cannot see a difference between her pupils and the color of her eyes.

Mary lived on about an acre. Her house was constructed of wood, concrete, and cinder blocks with four bedrooms and one bathroom. She also had two mangy-looking, emaciated dogs. At least we would not be having dog for lunch, least not those two dogs; they did not have enough meat on them.

Mary's backyard was filled with beautiful tall banana trees some stretched twenty feet in the air.

For a valley, the air in the Machakos area was clear and sweet—much different than the air in Nairobi. It felt great being outside. Father Pat excused himself to go back inside to use the bathroom. When Father Pat came out, I went in.

Since I have been home, I always get a laugh out of saying, "I can go to the bathroom anywhere; I've been to Africa." Mary's bathroom was a porcelain bowl buried in the ground with a drain hole in the middle. Sitting next to the bowl was a bucket filled with water and a big wooden spoon used to wash down the hole whatever was left in the bowl.

---

[11] A dirty kitchen is a cooking area that is detached from the house, usually with a dirt floor.

Lunch was served by Esther, and Mary made sure that she sat next to Father Pat. There were no surprises. Out came those same five Tupperware-like bowls: rice, beans, thick stew with peas and carrots, chicken, and that famous unidentifiable chewy meat with gravy.

Just before we left, Mary wanted to have her picture taken with Father Pat. We all went into the backyard where Father Pat and Mary stood next to a banana tree. Just before Esther snapped the photo, Father Pat pulled a banana leaf down across his face. So Esther's photo had Mary and a banana leaf wearing pants. For the photo I took, he played it straight.

Father Pat and Mary.

Mary was a gracious host, but we still had a couple of stops before we would be heading back to the convent. We promised Mary that on our next trip, we would come out to see her farm. We then said our final good-bye to Agnes, who would stay in Machakos; and thus, we began the one-hour drive to Sowento.

Father Pat made the interesting observation that when *he* sat in the front seat of the car, the talk was all about the church and spiritual issues. When *I* sat in the front seat, the talk was all politics. Kenya was a developing democracy, and I was very interested in its progress.

It was evident that the Moi government had let the infrastructure of Kenya fall completely apart. It had been years since any serious roadwork had been done. Social assistance by the government was nonexistent, and one might as well forget about a health care system. With the AIDS epidemic, there was no room for hospitals to treat much else.

I was talking to Tom about how voting was done in the country. There had not been a real election in over twenty-three years in Kenya. With the way people lived in the slums and in the countryside, there was no way to have accurate voter registration. I questioned Tom on how the government kept people from voting more than once and in different locations. Tom didn't seem to understand my puzzlement. He answered, "People just go to the voting place and vote." I decided to move on to something else.

There was a little town we passed through before we arrived at the slums. The town looked like the movie set from *Black Hawk Down*, with two buildings standing on one side of the street. The other side had remnants of buildings and a broken, buckled sidewalk. There was a store located on the bottom floor of a building that must have been built by the same guys who built the Leaning Tower of Pisa.

The unstable-looking building did not seem to deter the steady stream of men parading in and out of the store, going in empty-handed and coming out with fifty-pound bags of rice slung over their shoulders. This place looked as if a war was fought here. There actually was. It was a war on poverty, and poverty won.

Sowento is a small slum on the road back to Nairobi. After we left the main road, we drove about five miles down a one-lane dirt road that was bordered on the left by railroad tracks and on the right by houses with fenced-in backyards.

This road was a real kidney buster. Rocks and potholes covered every inch of the way. It took us about twenty minutes to travel about two miles. When we finally arrived in Sowento, we were greeted by a wonderful woman who was working with an industrious and entrepreneurial group of kids from the Sowento slums.

Leah Mbugua, fifty-five, lives just outside of Nairobi on a farm with her ninety-two-year-old mother. Leah is a member of the Kikuyu tribe who married a Maasai man and was extremely proud to tell us that she had a beautiful daughter named Njeri who lives in Hayward, California.[12]

The area just outside the Sowento slums was filled with white smoke that smelled like burning trash.

Playing under the drifting acrid white smoke were a group of preteen boys playing soccer with a ball they had made from old clothing, rags, and plastic shopping bags. One boy named John was an exceptionally good soccer player. He put on a great show for us. John could juggle that homemade soccer ball in the air with his feet; kick the ball high into the air; catch and balance it on the back of his neck; then flick it up over his head right back to his feet; and continue to juggle the ball with his feet, knees, and head. John was a natural. He liked to play keep away with all the other boys. He could keep the ball away from five or six other boys at once.

Leah called the boys to gather around Father Pat, and I took a picture. To my dismay, Father Pat told the boys that they could see their picture on my digital camera. So for the remainder of the time we stayed there, I had a gang of about eighteen boys following me around, trying to see themselves on a little one-and-a-half-inch screen on the back of my camera.

John works his magic.

---

12   Hayward, California, is located about one hour south of our hometown of American Canyon.

Father Pat had a great time clowning around with the kids. He would stand with his hands on top of his head, and the kids would do the same. He would put his hands on his hips, and the kids would do the same.

I met a boy named Mike. He was twenty-one years old and was a mentor to the young kids. He wanted to meet me because we had the same name. Mike was wearing a T-shirt proclaiming the slogan, "Kick the ball, kick AIDS, but don't pass it on to others." This was the theme of the youth in Sowento.

Mike asked if he could have his photo taken with me and if I could send him a copy. After I returned to California, I did send him a copy of the photo via Leah. I hope he received it. He told me that he lived in the slums for most of his life and saw no way out until last year when someone came up with the idea of burning trash for cash.

The kids of the slums had an ingenious and creative idea that not only solved a sanitation problem within the slums but also found a way to make enough money to help the families of the kids who participated in the program.

Mike and Mike.

Each day the younger kids would go around the slums and pick up all the garbage in the streets. They would then bring it to a large open area, located just outside the slums, and the older boys would separate the trash. Some of it was just burned off. But the degradable stuff was made into compost and sold to local shops and farmers.

This was a great project. It helped keep the slums clean, kept the kids busy, out of trouble; and it generated a few shillings.

Personally, I would have never considered turning trash into cash, but in this case, it was working quite well. It was an ingenious idea that used the available resources to solve several problems.

I whispered to Father Pat just loud enough for Sister Mary Theresa to hear me that I was getting hungry. The smell of all that burning trash must have triggered it.

Sister Mary Theresa butted in before Father Pat could comment, "Don't worry, Mike. In about an hour, we will be in Limuru Town to visit another of my pet projects: the archdiocese farm."

After saying good-bye to Mike and the other boys and promising Leah that we would contact her daughter in Hayward when we returned home, we headed to Limuru Town.

Lush green farmland greeted us. It reminded me of the farm that Karen Blixen described in her book *Out of Africa*. Acres of tea and coffee plants, and other fruits and vegetables lined the hillside. In the tea plantations, you could see little black heads popping up between the closely arranged plants as the workers dropped leaves into the baskets that they wore on their backs.

Arriving at the archdiocese farm, we were greeted by Father Al, who was in charge of the day-to-day operation. He had quite an assortment of vegetables cleaned and waiting for us.

We munched on carrots, celery, string beans, beets, and broccoli while Father Al and Sister Mary Theresa told us about the farm.

"We have three hundred acres here on the farm," Sister Mary Theresa said. "When I was a little girl growing up in Thika, my father worked on a tea farm and enjoyed it very much. It has always been my dream to have a tea farm someday." Apparently, Sister had many dreams as a kid. Remember when she told us that she wanted to be a police officer?

Anyway, she told us that the tea was planted about three years ago, and it takes about five years for the plants to mature enough to pick. "These plants are a little behind schedule because we have to water by hand."

"By hand?" I asked.

"Yes, we hand carry the water, bucket by bucket, from that reservoir at the bottom of the hill, put the water in that huge barrel at the top of the hill, and let gravity water the plants," she said.

Unbelievable, I thought. *Where is the Home Depot? A generator, water pump, and some PVC pipe, and we could get this thing going in no time.*

The farm had everything it needed except water, and you could tell the difference between the tea plants on the archdiocese farm and the tea plants on neighboring farms that were on a regular watering schedule. I wondered what the lack of water would do to the taste of the tea.

We had hoped that the archdiocese would be a leader in the community in the payment of wages, but we were disappointed to learn that the most the farmhands made was one hundred twenty shillings a day or about one dollar and fifty cents. When it is an employer's market, as it is in Kenya with 60 percent unemployment, employers can pay whatever they want. The church was no exception. If the workers don't like it, there are ten others waiting to take their jobs.

The one benefit they did have was that several of the farmworkers lived on the farm, and the others lived nearby so they did not have the cost of commuting. Many of the farmers were able to eat the food that they grew, so in comparison to others, they were doing well.

Perfectly balanced.

Sister Mary Theresa led us out into the field where they were growing broccoli and carrots. Heading toward us was a tall African woman wearing a bright wraparound skirt, and she was balancing a large basket on her head, which was full of carrots and string beans. I was mesmerized by the sight. She had perfect posture, and she showed so much confidence that the basket would stay put on her head.

I think I was more concerned than they were about the lack of water. It is such an abundant commodity at home. I had never thought twice about washing the driveway at home with copious amounts of water or taking a twenty-minute shower.

In Kenya, the people leave their supply of water up to the gods, and they seemed more than happy to do so.

Chapter 9

Snapshots

During our trip, there were many people we met and events that happened along the way that just didn't quite fit in the flow of the story. I would like to share them with you now.

Coincidence?

This occurred the day after Father Pat asked me to go to Kenya with him. I was digging around in our damp and dirty storage room, looking for something that would help my son with a school project; I came across a red leather-bound book, a first edition written by Sir Winston S. Churchill. When I got home, I placed the book on my dresser, and it faded once again out of memory.

While I was daydreaming during Sunday Mass, the title of that first-edition Churchill book just popped into my head: *My African Journey*.

The Rift Valley

The last full day in Kenya was spent on a short safari. We decided the day before that we had to see some of those *National Geographic* animals before we left Kenya. It was a welcomed break from all the sickness we had seen.

Early Thursday morning, we loaded up the Land Cruiser and headed to Lake Nakuru National Park. The journey through the Rift Valley was almost as exciting as the park itself because of all the stories I had read, before this trip, of the Leakey family's archeological discoveries.

Standing along the west side of Highway C65, on the eastern edge of the Rift Valley, gave me the eerie feeling that I had been there before. It was a feeling that had been bubbling just below the surface from the moment that I set foot in Kenya. It was all coming out now. Maybe it was more of wishful thinking than of anything else, but I had this immense feeling that I had bloodlines that came from this valley.

The Rift Valley holds significant historical importance. World-renowned anthropologist Dr. Richard Leaky and his family had made some amazing discoveries that point to the possibility that man evolved in the Rift Valley.

Rising before us, over nine thousand feet from the valley floor, was majestic Mount Longonot. A dormant young volcano, it looked very much like Diamond Head on Oahu, Hawaii. With the clouds drifting over the valley, it was an incredible sight to see the shadows dancing along its rim.

Majestic Mount Longonot.

Unfortunately, I did not find out until I got home that I should have read my guidebook a little closer. Mount Longonot was a national park, and the fifteen dollars the park service was charging to climb it would have been an inexpensive treat. Next trip, this will be on my to-do list.

At one point, after stopping to let a Maasai pass with his cows, I asked Tom to pull over; I had to get out and pick up a few rocks to take home with me—my own piece of the Rift Valley.

Nakuru

Traveling north on Road A109 for other forty-five minutes, we arrived in Nakuru thirsty and a little hungry; we stopped for a quick cup of coffee and a couple of bananas at a local hotel.

I purchased a local paper and sat at an outdoor table overlooking the town square and enjoyed the warming sun. Finding a local newspaper is something I like to do anywhere I travel. You can learn quite a bit in a short time from the local rag.

On the front cover was a story of two men who, the day before, had robbed a bank. A mob of several men and women chased the two men, who were carrying a large bag of money, into the parking lot right across the street from where we were sitting. The crowd beat the hell out of the two men and left them for the police. The money was never recovered. So was the crowd interested in justice, or were they just interested in their cut? Payment, I suppose, for catching the thieves.

After a couple of cups of coffee, we headed north to the national game reserve. It had an interesting pricing structure: three dollars for Kenyan residents, forty-five dollars for the rest of us.

The park was low-key. You just drive around on the trails and looked for animals. We did get to see a black rhino, which is very rare because it was nearly hunted into extinction by poachers interested in the professed aphrodisiac qualities of its horn.

A standoff with a water buffalo was the event of the day. We were traveling down a road, looking at these little deerlike animals called Kirk's Dik Dik, when a male water buffalo stepped out in the center of the trail, looked us straight in the eye, and refused to budge. The water buffalo is tremendously stubborn and is one of the most dangerous animals in Africa.

Water buffalo in Nakuru National Park.

After a five-minute standoff, Tom was getting a little nervous, and he was sure it was time to turn around. Tom was very careful, but the buffalo became annoyed with us anyway; and he chased us a few hundred feet back down the trail.

Lightning Can Make Your Skin Tingle

On our way out of the valley, just before we got back to the main road, it started to rain. I could imagine the natives dancing a happy dance in the valley and in Nairobi, where they had been praying for rain for months.

Later back at the convent, Father Pat and I were standing out on the walkway, enjoying a cocktail before dinner. All of a sudden, we heard a deafening crack, and everything in front of us turned blinding white; for a moment, we could not see anything else. The hair on the back of my neck and the hair on my arms stood straight up. I looked like Don King!

Immediately, we felt the pressure of the air rushing back to fill the hole that was made by the lightning bolt that hit several feet in front of us. It nearly knocked us down.

The good news was that neither one of us spilled a drop of our drinks. Without looking at each other or speaking a word, we quickly moved inside.

That lightning bolt knocked the power out at the convent, and it would not come back on for three days.

At six thirty the next morning, Father Pat was scheduled to say Mass at the chapel for the sisters. The power had not come back on, and the candles did not light up the chapel well enough for Father Pat to read the gospel. So he recited it from memory. I was rather impressed and told him later in the vestibule.

"That was not the gospel reading for today," he said. "I have one memorized just for emergencies, and since it was too dark to read from the book, I used that one."

A few of the sisters said that they were disappointed that the power did not come back on because they had a hard time seeing me. "In the dark," they said, "I looked as black as they were."

Those Damn Savages

After breakfast, we headed to the cathedral where Father Pat was scheduled to say Mass with the archbishop.

Just outside the St. Paul's Bookstore, located next to the cathedral, there was a white nun standing by herself.

"Is she American, or is she from Great Britain?" Father Pat asked.

"I don't know. Let me see her teeth first," I said, trying to make a joke about the crooked teeth of the English.

We were both wrong. She was from Italy, and she cracked us up, not because she was funny but because she was stupid.

"So, Sister Irene," Father Pat said, reading her name from the tag on her blouse, "fancy seeing another white face here in downtown Nairobi," Father Pat's humor was lost on the sister.

She retorted almost indignantly, "I've been here for three months, and I'm not feeling well; so I came to Nairobi to see a doctor."

I guessed that she was about sixty-five years old.

"So, Sister, what are you doing here in Kenya?" I jumped in.

"I was assigned to convert those savages," she said with a scrunched-up face. Her statement looked like it nearly put her face into spasms when she said it.

"The savages?" Father Pat and I asked almost in unison.

"Yes, you know, the Maasai. I was sent to convert the Maasai to Christianity. They are so immoral."

"Continue, Sister," Father Pat was now egging her on.

"Those Maasai! Did you know that they have more than one wife? They have sex with more than one woman!" She was nearly yelling now.

"I just don't know what to do. They never stay in one place. They are just savages. It's going to take the rest of my life to convert these savages."

"That's right," Father Pat added to her misery. "That plan always works—move in and shove Christianity right down the native's throats. It always works, doesn't it?"

Before the sister could take another shot at us, we both slid into the bookstore.

Separation of Church and State?

Before arriving in Kenya, we received an official letter inviting us to Kenya as the guests of Archbishop Ndingi. We actually hadn't received the letter until we arrived in Kenya, but at least, the letter had been written. It served no purpose except for the fact that Sister Mary Theresa thought that our visit was important enough to warrant an official invitation.

Everywhere we went, everyone said, "Oh, Archbishop Ndingi. He is a small man, you know."

I had heard that from so many people that I expected the guy to be about four feet tall. So when we finally met him, I was surprised to see that he was about five feet five—not a small man at all.

The day before we met with the archbishop, we saw a full-page ad in the local newspaper, the *Daily Nation*, featuring the archbishop speaking about AIDS.

The last line of the ad said, "Abstinence is the best way to prevent AIDS, but if you must have sex, use a condom."

"Wow," Father Pat and I both said. Here is an enlightened archbishop. Needless to say that while we were munching on lamb and sweet potatoes at lunch with the archbishop, we brought up the ad; and before we could compliment him on his statement, he interrupted us by saying, "I called the newspaper personally and told them that they better print a retraction and an apology because I never mentioned anything about using a condom."

"Darn," I said to Father Pat. What a missed opportunity.

But this "small man" was tough and had been causing the government of Kenya problems for forty years.

He was appointed bishop at the tender age of eighteen! That is unheard of in the Catholic Church. Usually, if a person becomes a bishop in their forties, they are considered fortunate. During the Moi regime, Archbishop Ndingi was banished from Nairobi for his constant protesting against the government for their policies or, should I say, lack of policies concerning human rights and the poor.

The archbishop explained to us that Moi put so much pressure on the church that he was sent to Nakuru and was told not to set foot in Nairobi. Several years later, Bishop Ndingi was allowed to return to Nairobi by the government only if he agreed to keep his criticism of the government to himself. Of course, Archbishop Ndingi did not hold up his end of the bargain and still spoke out at every opportunity.

While we were in Kenya, the country was celebrating its first year under a freely elected, democratic government and was in the process of writing a new constitution. Archbishop Ndingi was on the committee in charge of that history-making task.

He held the process up for several weeks because he said that there were not enough social programs guaranteed in the new constitution, and he could not support it.

Make no mistake about it. From the reaction we received from AK-47 army man at the airport when we arrived in Kenya to hearing and reading about how Archbishop Ndingi was able to hold up the constitutional congress, he was far from being a small man.

The Faithful

We had made it through two grueling and emotional weeks. It was Friday, and we would be flying home that night. Father

Agnes, Father Pat, Archbishop Ndingi, Sister Mary Theresa, and me.

Pat was excited that he was going to celebrate noontime Mass with Archbishop Ndingi. He wanted me to make sure I took many pictures of him and the archbishop together at the alter.

As I said before, one of the great things about the Catholic Mass is that the process and procedures are the same all over the world. So if you can say Mass in California, you can say Mass in Africa, no problem.

Father Pat looked like he was enjoying himself. What stunned us both was that there were over one thousand people attending the Mass. This was unbelievable. I had never seen such a crowd for a noontime Mass before.

Afterward, we were told that most businesses adjust their lunch hour so their employees could attend Mass. Could you imagine that ever happening in the United States?

Father Pat at Holy Family Cathedral, downtown Nairobi.

Pig Farmers

Father Pat and I were so pleased and proud that we had made such good friends with our driver Tom Wahome. He was more than just a driver to us. He became our brother. We, unfortunately, did not get a chance to meet his daughters Scholastica and Rosslyn or his wife, Idah. On our next trip, I hope to spend a few days in Tom's home to get to know his family.

I said we were so proud of our relationship because if Tom had a need, he was not too proud, embarrassed, or shy to ask us.

With such high unemployment and poverty in Kenya, it not only affects one's ability to feed one's family, but it also affects the moral and mental health of one's family.

Tom—being the father, husband, and provider that he is—knew he had to do something for Idah. She had a degree in agriculture but could not find work or a way to apply her training. He told us that her lack of financial contribution to the family was weighing heavily on her.

About two months after our return home, Father Pat received a letter from Tom, explaining the situation with his wife and asking us for a favor. Tom had this great idea that Idah could become a pig farmer. It would give her something to do, and she could then contribute to the financial status of the family. "It would be big boost to her," Tom said.

The problem was they needed about one thousand two hundred dollars to buy the pigs, build a suitable sty for them to live, and provide food.

Without even blinking an eye, Father Pat went directly to the bank and wired the money to Tom. Now Father Pat calls himself a pig farm co-owner with Idah in Kenya.

The family now has a sow, and their farm is self-sustaining.

Gift to the Airport

One of the pieces I purchased in Machakos was a beautiful hand-carved walking cane. It was carved from olive wood and had a round handle; and along the shaft were carvings of elephants, rhinos, giraffe, and water buffalo. When the woman in the shop cleaned it with some sort of oil, it brought out the natural grain of the wood. It was beautiful. I could not wait to get it home and show it to my wife, Patti. But it never made it home.

I was hoping that the cane would fit in my suitcase, but it was about three inches too long, and I had to hand carry it through the airport.

Inside Nairobi airport, I was walking around with my cane wrapped in a large sheet of butcher paper. It caused quite a stir with one of those green army men I wrote about earlier. It took me a few minutes to understand why my package was causing such a commotion. It was slightly funny afterward; but when the army man asked me to hand it to him, I realized that, wrapped in butcher paper, it looked exactly like a rifle. I breathed a sigh of relief when the green army man escorted me to the ticket counter and told the woman that I could carry it on the flight. But the woman at the boarding gate saw things a little differently, and she made me check it in as luggage. I should have pretended that I needed it to walk. When I checked it in with the woman at the gate, it was the last I saw of it.

Chapter 10

Final Thoughts

Standing, as I did, in January of 2004, on the rim of the Great Rift Valley, I felt deep in my soul a stirring that could have only come from the knowledge that I came from there. We all came from somewhere in that valley.

It was easy to imagine the creatures, before man first stood tall, living the high-life, grazing on lush green trees and tasty shrubs. When man evolved from that knuckle-dragging, hairy creature about one hundred thousand years ago, he moved out of the valley and migrated all over the world. It was those hairy, thick-foreheaded *Homo sapiens* who were our brothers.

Standing on that rim, filling my lungs full of fresh Kenyan air, was the exact moment that I fell in love with Kenya. This was the defining moment of my trip. I was filled with a deep sense of being home.

It is irritating to me that Africa has become the "in place." The popular media, Hollywood actors, and well-meaning politicians tell us that if we have a conscious, we should be concerned with the plight of the Africans.

It seems to me that Africa has become the place in the world that if we want to feel good, we can give money to the many different nonprofit organizations supporting Africa and then pound our puffy chests (or hairy chest, in my case) with our fist and say, "I feel good today. I fed an African"—not knowing and, in a sense, not caring how our money was actually spent. We are allowing ourselves to become part of the problem.

After British colonial rule, Kenya was left to self-government. It was during this period of time that the stage was set for corruption. History has shown us over and over again, especially in sub-Saharan Africa, that one cannot expect to suppress a people, treat those people like slaves, and then suddenly leave them and expect those same people to form a fair and equitable government. Kenya had over seventy different tribes at the time the British left, all with the idea that they should be ruling the country.

The world has spent billions in sub-Saharan Africa, and except in the country of South Africa, the people are not much better off.

In Kenya, the money has been siphoned off to the highest government officials; the money that has trickled down has been in the form of handouts. Give-away programs have created a climate of lazy, untrained, and uneducated people. These people have come to rely on those programs and have become virtual slaves to them. There is no training, no investment in the future, and no investment in personal growth. This is a toxic and deadly formula.

Our brothers and sisters in Kenya are an intelligent people, trying to dig themselves out of a huge hole created by a vicious and corrupt dictatorship. They are attempting to catch up with an ever-changing, materialistic world.

Materialism is everywhere. In a country where the average salary is about three hundred sixty dollars a year and where the large majority of people can only afford to purchase clothing that has been rejected by the Salvation Army or Goodwill in the United States, they are bombarded with materialism. The city is littered with billboard and the sound of ghetto blasters promoting the American lifestyle.

Although there are a few local television and radio stations, much of the programming comes from Great Britain and the United States. The youth of Kenya are teased, just like our kids are teased, with advertising designed to tickle their materialistic vanities.

The ads tell the youth that they can't be cool unless they have a pair of eighty-dollar Nike basketball shoes, a sixty-dollar pair of pants, or drive an eighty-thousand-dollar Mercedes Benz. Does this sound familiar? This is Western advertising at its worst, and it has created a huge problem within the Kenyan family structure. Many kids feel trapped and rebel against the tribal traditions of their parents and grandparents. They venture out, looking for the quick dollar and find that a life of selling drugs and committing crimes is able to provide quick cash and a sense of monetary wealth, at least for the short term.

Nice clothes, a nice car, and a comfortable life are some things that all humans strive for; but when one is from Kenya, living on a budget of a dollar a day and one is not sure where one's next meal is coming from, the perceived glamour from crime and corruption becomes too hard to resist.

As I mentioned earlier in the book, the Kenyans have put a great deal of hope in their government. I worry that their trust has been misplaced. This is because of the handout mentality that has been created over the last forty-plus years. The Kenyans are waiting for the government to lift them out of poverty. Personal and societal change can only come when the people of Kenya level the playing field by ending corruption in the court system. Corrupt courts allow the few with wealth to rule the country. Money speaks loudly in the third world.

Government is never the solution. The people of Kenya do have a sense of fairness; but they have lived so long under an oppressive, corrupt government that it is understandable to me that the people of Kenya believe that if their government got them into this mess, then their government can get them out of this mess too!

The statement that I heard over and over again "When the new government helps us out" stills rings painfully in my ear. The entire idea is misguided and a lie.

*　　*　　*

The last night Father Pat and I spent in Kenya, he said to me, "Wouldn't you feel like shit if we walked away from here and did nothing?"

We were at the end of our trip, and I was ready to come home. My senses were on overload; this had been an extremely emotional experience. Each night, my dreams were filled with dread and despair. I had dreams of sick children, children sniffing glue, teenage prostitutes, and death from AIDS. I had to get away from it to allow myself to process all that I had seen.

When we returned home, through a series of e-mails, we had Sister Mary Theresa and Sister Christine invite girls living on the streets of Nairobi who showed a desire to get off the streets to make African-style clothing and trinkets. The idea was that we could solicit donations from the people of our parish for the items and send the money back to the sisters to be used to fund some sort of street-children program.

From this came the Cardinal Maurice Otunga[13] Empowerment Center for Girls. The center is a live-in school and training center for teenage girls who desire to get away from the prostitution, crime, and rape of the streets of Nairobi. From the original donations we were able to collect, the sisters were able to house and teach fifteen girls. After a second shipment of handmade clothing, the donations we collected allowed the sisters to increase the numbers at the center to seventy eight.

This is not a handout program. The girls have to want to be there. To receive the benefits of a roof over their head, three meals a day, safety, and a solid education, they have to put in the effort to learn and to take care of each other. They have to earn the right to be there. This idea was very attractive to Father Pat and me because we did not want to contribute to the overall problem but wanted to train young people so that someday they could contribute to solving the problems of the people of Kenya.

I have been asked, "What about the boys?" Girls are especially susceptible to violence and brutality in the streets of Kenya. Women are not treated as equals;

---

[13] Cardinal Maurice Otunga was the much-beloved cardinal of Kenya who died in September 2003.

they are treated as possessions and things to be used. Being beaten, raped, becoming pregnant, and being exposed to HIV are everyday horrors to girls on the streets.

*   *   *

At a recent fund-raiser we hosted for the street kids of Nairobi along with two other local churches, I was introduced by a member of a black Baptist Church to the gathering. She said, "I was trying to figure out what this white boy was going to tell me about Africa. But after just a few minutes, I could tell that he knew what he was talking about."

Her comments drew quite a laugh from the one-hundred-or-so people that had gathered for the event. But it underscored an important issue. The problems in Africa are not black problems and they are not white problems. They are human problems.

It is so important for the reader to understand that the work we are doing in Africa is not from just another guilt-filled white guy trying to make things right or a white guy feeling sorry for the poor black people of Africa.

This work and book is the extension of my belief that the human race is like a chain; we are only as strong as our weakest link. The people of Africa are the weakest link.

What You Can Do to Help

If you would like to help the Street Kids of Nairobi Project or the girls of the Cardinal Maurice Otunga Empowerment Center, you can send a check to

> Nairobi Street Kids Project
> c/o Holy Family Parish,
> 402 Donaldson Way, American Canyon CA 94503

Make your check payable to the Holy Family Parish with "Nairobi Street Kids" written in the memo section of your check.

You may also contact me at the following e-mail address:

michaelschneiders@yahoo.com

A portion of the profits from the sale of this book will go directly to the Nairobi Street Kids Project.